Irish Curses,
Blessings, and Toasts

Irish Curses, Blessings, and Toasts

A Little Book of Wit, Wisdom, and Whimsy

NICHOLAS NIGRO

HAMPTON ROADS

Cover design by Jim Warner
Cover illustration: Getty Images © Exxorian
Interior design by Deborah Dutton
Typeset in Bembo

Hampton Roads Publishing Company, Inc.
Charlottesville, VA 22906
Distributed by Red Wheel/Weiser, LLC
www.redwheelweiser.com

Sign up for our newsletter and special offers by going to
www.redwheelweiser.com/newsletter.

ISBN: 978-1-57174-828-7
Library of Congress Cataloging-in-Publication Data available upon request

Printed in Canada
MAR

10 9 8 7 6 5 4 3 2 1

To Pat Mitchell's Kingsbridge

Contents

Introduction

The Irish people have a way with words. In the pantheon of literary giants, Irish writers have left their mark and then some. From Oscar Wilde to James Joyce, Samuel Beckett to Brendan Behan, Irish wordsmiths have simultaneously reshaped and modernized literature. But it isn't just the literary-endowed who appreciate the width and breadth of language and the unique power of words; it's Irish men and women of all ages and in all parts of the world.

Indeed, the Irish are renowned for their unrivaled capacity to spin a yarn and tell a story. They have a singular gift for gab and delight in the art of conversation. Being Irish means finding both humor and insight on life's roller coaster ride of highs and lows. Irish novelist and playwright Edna O'Brien once remarked, "When anyone asks me about the

Irish character, I say look at the trees: maimed, stark, and misshapen, but ferociously tenacious."

Undeniably, the Irish narrative is chock-full of wit, fellowship, and merriment, but it is also deeply rooted in a revolutionary past of severe hardship. There is, too, a tremendous pride in the Irish national identity—one that transcends continents and generations. Whether those of Irish ancestry live in Ireland itself, or thousands of miles across the ocean in North America, they venerate their glorious green homeland. They never forget who they are or where they came from. Strong familial and cultural bonds ensure that nobody of Irish ancestry is forgotten, even long after their deaths.

Rightly so, it has been said that the Irish love nothing more than talking about being Irish and reaching into their treasure trove of words and sentiments for any and all occasions. *Irish Curses, Blessings, and Toasts* gathers together and neatly categorizes this treasure trove of materials in one entertaining and informative volume.

CHAPTER ONE

Blessings and Toasts

People from all parts of the world appreciate and appropriate Irish blessings and toasts. It's a testament to the emotions they engender, which run a wide gamut. Many of the blessings and toasts are heartfelt and touching, while others—it's the Irish after all— are distinctly droll and laugh-out-loud entertaining.

May the road rise to meet you.
May the wind be always at your back.
May the sun shine warm upon your face
And rains fall soft upon your fields.
And until we meet again,
May God hold you in the hollow of His hand.

May your joys be as deep as the oceans,
Your troubles as light as its foam,
And may you find sweet peace of mind
Wherever you may roam.

May you have enough happiness to keep you sweet,
Enough trials to keep you strong,
Enough sorrow to keep you human,
Enough hope to keep you happy,
Enough failure to keep you humble,
Enough success to keep you eager,
Enough wealth to meet your needs,
Enough enthusiasm to look forward,
Enough friends to give you comfort,
Enough faith to banish depression,
And one thing more,
Enough determination to make
Each day better than yesterday.

May your day be touched by a bit of Irish luck,
Brightened by a song in your heart,
And warmed by the smiles of the people you love.

May the lilt of Irish laughter
Lighten every load.
May the mist of Irish magic
Shorten every road.
And may all your friends remember
All the favors you are owed.

May the power of God guide you,
The might of God uphold you,
The wisdom of God teach you,
The eye of God watch over you,
The ear of God hear you,
The word of God give you speech,
The hand of God protect you,
The way of God go before you,
The shield of God shelter you.

May you have all the happiness
And luck that life can hold.
And at the end of all your rainbows
May you find a pot of gold.

May your mornings bring joy
And your evenings bring peace.
May your troubles grow less
As your blessings increase.

May you have:
A world of wishes at your
    command,
God and his angels close
    to hand,
Friends and family their
    love impart,
And Irish blessings in your heart.

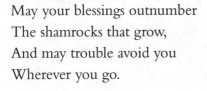

May your blessings outnumber
The shamrocks that grow,
And may trouble avoid you
Wherever you go.

May your troubles be less
And your blessings be more,
And nothing but happiness
Come through your door.

May your thoughts be as glad as the shamrocks,
May your heart be as light as a song,
May each day bring you bright, happy hours
That stay with you all the year long.

May your neighbors respect you,
Troubles neglect you,
The angels protect you,
And Heaven accept you.

May you always have
Walls for the winds,
A roof for the rain,
Tea beside the fire,
Laughter to cheer you,
Those you love near you,
And all your heart might desire.

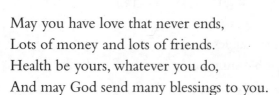

May you have love that never ends,
Lots of money and lots of friends.
Health be yours, whatever you do,
And may God send many blessings to you.

May the sun shine all day long,
Everything go right and nothing
    wrong.
May those you love bring love
    back to you,
And may all the wishes you wish
    come true.

May the sound of happy music
And the lilt of Irish laughter,
Fill your heart with gladness
That stays forever after.

May you
Live long,
Die happy,
And rate a mansion in Heaven.

May you always walk in sunshine,
May you never want for more.
May Irish angels rest their wings
Right beside your door.

May the blessing of the rain be on you,
The soft sweet rain.
May it fall upon your spirit
So that all the little flowers may spring up
And shed their sweetness on the air.
May the blessing of the great rains be on you.
May they beat upon your spirit
And wash it fair and clean,
And leave there many a shining pool
Where the blue of Heaven shines,
And sometimes a star.

May God grant you many years to live,
For sure He must be knowing.
The earth has angels all too few
And Heaven is overflowing.

May you have the hindsight to know where you've
    been,
The foresight to know where you're going,
And the insight to know when you're going too far.

May God grant you always
A sunbeam to warm you,
A moonbeam to charm you,
A sheltering angel, so nothing can harm you.

May peace and plenty bless your world
With joy that long endures.
May all life's passing seasons
Bring the best to you and yours.

Always remember to forget
The things that made you sad,
But never forget to remember
The things that made you glad.
Always remember to forget
The friends that proved untrue,
But never forget to remember
Those that have stuck by you.
Always remember to forget
The troubles that passed away,
But never forget to remember
The blessings that come each day.

May you have warm words on a cold evening,
A full moon on a dark night,
And the road downhill
All the way to your door.

May the morning sun stir you from the bed,
May the winds of March move you on the road,
May the rains of April renew you strength,
May the flowers of May captivate your sight,
May summer heat inflame your zeal,
May autumn color stimulate your dreams,
May the silver moon make you wiser yet,
May you never be with yourself content,
May Jesus and Mary keep you young,
Full of life and laughter and an Irish song.

May your faith be strong as a mountain wall
And subtle as the early morning mists.
May you believe that God's power conquers all
And his love through trouble and pain persists.
May your faith soar like a multi-colored bird
And shine brighter than the blinding desert sun.
Because you know your prayers are ever heard
And Jesus waits when the final day is done.
And may God bless you,
The Father who rules the starry skies,
The Son who rose from the dead,
And the Spirit who comes in hope.

May the autumn leaves carpet beneath your feet
And the angels lead you through the classday maze.
May your homecoming time be extra sweet
And your heart warm with Indian summer days.
Like Jesus, may you grow in wisdom, age, and grace,
May you learn to read and write and think and
     sing,
May you swiftly run in knowledge's rapid race
And may God's kind love to all your roommates
     bring.

Dance as if no one were watching,
Sing as if no one were listening,
And live every day as if it were your last.

Here's a health to all those that we love.
Here's a health to all those that love us.
Here's a health to all those that love them.

Here's to health, peace, and prosperity.
May the flower of love never be nipped
By the frost of disappointment,
Nor the shadow of grief
Fall among your family and friends.

Like the gold of the sun,
Like the light of the day,
May the luck of the Irish
Shine bright on your way.
Like the glow of a star
And the lilt of a song,
May these be your joys
All your life long.

Bless the house
And bless the hearth.
Bless the work
And bless all here.
May your faith be strong,
May your heart be true,
And the devil n'er
Make a liar of you.

May you be blessed with
Warmth in your home,
Love in your heart,
Peace in your soul,
And joy in your life.

May your pockets be heavy and your heart be light.
May good luck pursue you each morning and
    night.

For each petal on the shamrock,
This brings a wish your way.
Good health, good luck, and happiness
For today and every day.

Here's that we may always have
A clean shirt,
A clean conscience,
And a guinea in our pocket.

May the frost never afflict your spuds,
May the outside leaves of your cabbage
    always be free from worms,
May the crow never pick
    your haystack,
And may your donkey always
    be in foal.

May the embers from the open hearth warm your
    hands,
May the sun's rays from the Irish sky warm your
    face,
May the children's bright smiles warm your heart,
And may the everlasting love I give you warm your
    soul.

May you always have work for your hands to do,
May your pockets hold always a coin or two,
May the sun shine bright on your windowpane,
May the rainbow be certain to follow each rain,
May the hand of a friend always be near you,
And may God fill your heart with gladness to cheer
    you.

Leprechauns, castles, good luck, and laughter,
Lullabies, dreams, and love ever after.
Poems and songs with pipes and drums,
A thousand welcomes when anyone comes.

Wishing you a rainbow
For sunlight after showers,
Miles and miles of Irish smiles
For golden happy hours.
Shamrocks at your doorway
For luck and laughter too,
And a host of friends that
    never ends
Each day your whole life
    through.

May the good saints protect you
And bless you today.
And may troubles ignore you,
Each step of the way.

As the Lord sent His disciples into the world
And assured them He would be with them until
   the end of time,
So, too, may the Holy Spirit be with you and yours
As you share the word of God's love
With all you meet along the road.

Whenever there is happiness
Hope you'll be there too.
Wherever there are friendly smiles
Hope they'll smile on you.
Whenever there is sunshine,
Hope it shines especially for you,
To make each day for you as bright as it can be.

May you taste the sweetest pleasures
That fortune ere bestowed,
And may all your friends remember
All the favors you are owed.

May joy and peace surround you,
Contentment latch your door,
And happiness be with you now,
And bless you evermore.

May good luck be your friend
In whatever you do.
And may trouble be always
A stranger to you.

These things, I warmly wish
    for you:
Someone to love,
Some work to do,
A bit of o' sun,
A bit o' cheer,
And a guardian angel
    always near.

May brooks and trees and singing hills
Join in the chorus too.
And may every gentle wind that blows
Send happiness to you.

Lucky stars above you,
Sunshine on your way,
Many friends to love you,
Joy in work and play.
Laughter to outweigh each care,
In your heart a song,
And gladness waiting everywhere
All your whole life long.

When the first light of sun,
Bless you.
When the long day is done,
Bless you.
In your smiles and your tears,
Bless you.
Through each day of your years,
Bless you.

May a rainbow gladden your eyes,
May soft winds freshen your spirit,
May sunshine brighten your heart,
May the burdens of the day rest lightly upon you,
And may God enfold you
In the mantle of his love.

May you enjoy the four greatest blessings:
Honest work to occupy you,
A hearty appetite to sustain you,
A good woman to love you,
And a wink from the God above.

May the wings of the butterfly kiss the sun
And find your shoulder to light on,
To bring you luck, happiness, and riches,
Today, tomorrow, and beyond.

May you live a long life
Full of gladness and health,
With a pocket full of gold
As the least of your wealth.
May the dreams you hold dearest,
Be those which come true,
The kindness you spread,
Keep returning to you.

May the friendships you make,
Be those which endure,
And all of your gray clouds
Be small ones for sure.
And trusting in Him
To Whom we all pray,
May a song fill your heart
Every step of the way.

May God be with you and bless you,
May you see your children's children,
May you be poor in misfortune, rich in blessings,
And may you know nothing but happiness
From this day forward.

May you live as long as you want
And never want as long as you live.

May your heart be light and happy,
May your smile be big and wide,
And may your pockets always have a coin or two
    inside.

May you have food and raiment,
A soft pillow for your head.
May you be forty years in
    Heaven
Before the devil knows
    you're dead.

May the God of the dawn awaken you,
May the God of sunrise stir you up,
May the God of morning bless your work,
May the God of noon renew your strength,
May the God of sunset bring you home,
May the God of dusk soothe your soul,
May the God of night bring you rest.

May your days be many
And your troubles be few,
May all of God's blessings descend upon you.
May peace be within you,
May your heart be strong,
May you find what you're seeking
Wherever you roam.

May your glass be ever full,
May the roof over your head be always strong,
And may you be in Heaven half an hour
Before the devil knows you're dead.

May your joys be as bright as the morning
And your sorrows merely be shadows that fade
In the sunlight of love.

May the blessing of God's soft rain be on you,
Falling gently on your head,
Refreshing your soul with the sweetness
Of summer flowers newly blooming.

May the blessings of each day be the blessings you
    need most.
May the most you wish for be the least you get.
May the Lord keep you in His Hand
And never close His fist too tight.

May God give you
For every storm, a rainbow,
For every tear, a smile,
For every care, a promise,
And a blessing in each trial.
For every problem life sends,
A faithful friend to share,
For every sigh, a sweet song,
And an answer for each prayer.

May the blessing of light be upon you:
Light on the outside,
Light on the inside.
With God's sunlight shining on you,
May your heart glow with warmth
Like a turf fire that welcomes friends and strangers
    alike.
May the light of the Lord shine from your eyes
Like a candle in the window
Welcoming the weary traveler.

May the sun shine all day long,
Everything go right
And nothing wrong.
May those you love
Bring love back to you,
And may all the wishes
You wish come true.

May love and laughter light your days
And warm your heart and home.
May good and faithful friends be yours
Wherever you may roam.
May peace and plenty bless your world
With joy that long endures.
May all life's passing seasons
Bring the best to you and yours.

The love and affection of the angels be to you,
The love and affection of the saints be to you,
The love and affection of Heaven be to you,
To guard and to cherish you.
May God shield you on every step,
May He aid you on every path,
And may He hold you safe on every slope,
On every hill and on every plain.
In this Irish home
May these walls be filled with laughter,
May it reach from floor to rafter,
May the roof keep out the rain,
May sunshine warm each windowpane,
And may the door be open wide
To let the Good Lord's love inside.

May you never find trouble
All crowdin' and shovin'.
But always good fortune,
All smilin' and lovin'.

May brooks and trees
And singing hills
Join in the chorus too,
And every gentle wind that blows
Send happiness to you.

Come and take potluck with me.
My heart is warm,
My friendship's free.

May good fortune be yours.
May your joys never end.

May your blessings be many,
The sunshine above you,
Your life bring you gladness,
And always God love you.

Grant me a sense of humor, Lord,
The saving grace to see a joke,
To win some happiness from life,
And pass it on to other folk.

Let's put on our dancin' shoes
And wear our shamrocks green,
And toast our friends both here and there
And everywhere between.

The future is not ours to know
And it may never be,
So let us live and give our best
And give it lavishly.

I asked a leprechaun to bring
A pot of gold to you.
I asked a fiddler if he'd play
Your favorite ditty too.
I asked the saints to walk
    with you
Each step along the way.
And now I'm asking you
To have a very happy day.

Near a misty stream in Ireland
In the hollow of a tree
Live mystical, magical leprechauns
Who are clever as can be.
With their pointed ears and turned up toes
And little coats of green,
The leprechauns busily make their shoes
And try hard not to be seen.
Only those who really believe
Have seen these little elves,
And if we are all believers
We can surely see for ourselves.

Long live the Irish!
Long live their cheer!
Long live our friendship
Year after year!

May God guard you
Through each day and night
And ever watch above you.
God smile on everything you do,
God go with you,
God love you.

There's much in the Irish names,
Kilkenny, Tipperary.
There's beauty in the countryside,
From Cork to Londonderry.
And whoever makes his earthly home
Close to the Irish sod
Has found a bit of Heaven
And walks hand in hand with God.

Wishing you always
A bright sky above,
The pleasure of doing
The things that you love.
God's blessing around you,
His light from on high
And deeper contentment
As each day goes by.

May God in His wisdom and infinite love
Look down on you always from Heaven above.
May He send you good fortune, contentment,
   and peace.
And may all your blessings forever increase.

God needed laughter in the world,
So he made the Irish race.
For they can meet life with a smile
And turn a happy face.

May God bless you now and always
With the gift of Irish cheer,
So you will have a happy heart
Every day and all year.

Here's a special Irish wish,
You can hear it in Cork or Kerry:
God bless yourself,
God bless your house,
And may your days be merry.

I wish you lots of good luck
No matter what the day.
I wish you lots of sunshine
And not a bit of gray.
I wish you lots of laughter
And never one wee sigh.
And I hope no gift of fortune
May ever pass you by.

Irish wishes are prayers indeed,
And this is especially true,
When the Irish wishes are made and sent
On any day to you.

All the little leprechauns
In Ireland's sunny isle
Couldn't bring you all the luck
I'm wishing you the while.

May you always be wearing
    a big, happy smile
And really enjoying each day.
And may all the luck of the
    Emerald Isle
Always be coming your way.

Sure and this just isn't blarney
For what I say is true.
The luck of the Irish was with me
The day that I met you.

There's the joy of old Killarney
In these wishes meant for you.
There's a bit of Irish blarney,
There's a touch of magic too.
There's a wish for lots of laughter
And good luck, be sure of that.
And a wish that all you're wishing
May come true in no time flat.

May good luck befriend you
And kind fortune send you
Whatever your heart may be wishin'.
May good friends be near you
To gladden and cheer you
And help you attain each ambition.

Wishing you joys that are lasting and true,
A heart that's not troubled or gray,
Friends who will travel life's pathway with you
And the luck of the Irish each day.

May all your skies be blue ones,
May all your dreams be seen,
May all your friends be true ones,
And all your joys complete.
May happiness and laughter
Fill all your days for you.
Today and ever after
May all your dreams come true.

Irish luck's proverbial.
It never fails, they say,
And that's the kind I'm wishin' you
With all my heart today.
And faith, that's not the half of it,
I wish you fun and laughter,
Good friends and health and happiness
Today and ever after.

They talk of the luck of the Irish,
The magic of the shamrocks too,
But sure and it's more than Irish luck
To be knowing someone like you.

Like the shamrocks of Old Ireland,
May your joys grow all year through,
And Irish luck and laughter
Be a part of all you do.

Wishing you lots of Irish luck
And joy in whatever life sends.
Liking you always because you are you
And happy because we are friends.

'Tis the best of good fortune
I hope you will know.
And the best of good cheer
As the years come and go.
Good friends ever near you,
Good luck to you too,
And good health to enjoy
All I'm wishing you.

It's a bit o' Irish luck
With all its fun and cheer
That's wished for you not just today
But every day of the year.

May the luck of the Irish
Lead to happiest heights,
And the highway you travel
Be lined with green lights.
Wherever you go and whatever you do,
May the luck of the Irish be there with you.

Here's wishing you the tops o' life
Without a single tumble.
Here's wishing you the smiles o' life
And not a single grumble.
Here's wishing you the best o' life
And not a flaw about it.
Here's wishing you all the joy in life
And not a day without it.

You've heard of the luck o' the Irish.
It's the best in the world, no end.
And my own is the luck o' the Irish
In havin' you for a friend.

I'm wishing you joy,
I'll be havin' you know,
And the luck o' the Irish
Wherever you go.

To wish you top of the morning
The best that any day sends.
To wish you the cheer at noontime
That comes with the thought of friends.
And when the evening shadows
Full lengthening o'er the way,
To wish you the heart's contentment
That comes with the perfect day.

Many blessings to cheer you
Each day the year through,
And the luck of the Irish
In all that you do.

You'd have to look the world around
From here to old Killarney
To find someone as nice as you
And that's no Irish blarney.

God bless you—now and always—
With the gift of Irish cheer.
God give to you a happy heart
And keep you through the year.

A wish that every day for you
Will be happy from the start.
And may you always have good luck
And a song within your heart.

They say the Irish are the luckiest
Or so I have been told,
Because at every rainbow's end
They find a pot of gold.
So somewhere deep inside me
I must be Irish too,
For waiting at my rainbow's end
I luckily found you.

May leprechauns strew happiness
Wherever you walk each day,
And Irish angels smile on you
All along the way.

Here's a wish for a day
That's lucky all through
From the likes o' me
To the likes o' you.

As sure as there are leprechauns
To make a wish come true,
'Tis nothing but the happiest
Of days I'm wishing you.

May joy be your companion
Through each and every day
Bringing lots of Irish luck
And happiness your way.

Here's hoping your face
Is wearing a smile
As cheery and bright
As the old Emerald Isle.
And may a full measure
Of Irish luck too
Make each day of the year
A grand one for you.

'Tis glad I am
And glad I'll be
Knowin' you like
The likes o' me.

Irish Curses, Blessings, and Toasts

May your days be as sparkling
As an Irish smile,
The dew on a shamrock
And the Emerald Isle.

Good times,
Good friends,
Good health to you
And the luck of the Irish
In all that you do.

An Irish wish from the heart of a friend:
May good fortune be yours,
May your joys never end.

May your days be as bright
As the lakes of Killarney,
Your spirits be high
As the blue Irish sky.
May you walk in the path
Where the shamrocks are growin'
And blessing to you
For a wonderful day.

Leprechauns, castles, good luck, and laughter,
Lullabies, dreams, and love ever after.
Poems and songs with pipes and drums,
A thousand welcomes when anyone comes.

May you have these:
The bright warm sun of happiness,
The soft cool shade of joy,
And many pleasures your whole life through.

May you have many pleasant hours
To melt your cares away,
And the warmth of Irish laughter
To bring gladness to each day.

May your heart be light and happy,
May your smile be big and wide,
And may your pockets always have
A tinkle of gold inside.

May you have many blessings
And wherever your path may wind,
May every day that's coming
Be the bright and happy kind.

May you have these blessings:
Good health to make life enjoyable,
Good fortune to make it bright,
And lots of happiness always
With everything going just right.

Catch the moments as they fly
And use them as ye ought man.
Believe me happiness is shy
And comes not aye when sought man.

May you never forget
What is worth remembering,
Or remember what is best forgotten.

Sláinte go saol agat,
Bean ar do mhian agat.
Leanbh gach blian agat,
is solas na bhflaitheas tareis antsail seo agat.
Health for life to you,
A wife of your choice to you,
Land without rent to you,
A child every year to you,
And the light of Heaven after this world for you.

Pithy Toasts

Sláinte!
Health!

Sláinte mhath!
Good health!

Sláinte mhor!
Great health!

Slàinte mhor a h-uile là a chi 's nach fhaic!
Great health to you every day I see you and every
day I don't!

Sláinte chuig na fir, agus go mairfidh na mná go deo!
Health to the men, and may the women live forever!

Faol saol agat, gob fliuch, agus bás in Éirinn.
Long life to you, a wet mouth, and death in Ireland.

On earth and on sea until you are home again.

I wish you all you could wish for yourself.

May I see you gray and combing your grandchildren's hair.

May your right hand always be stretched out in friendship and never in want.

May God bring good health to your enemies' enemies.

May the dust of your carriage blind the eyes of your foe.

May misfortune follow you all the days of your life and never catch up.

May the roof above us never fall in, and may we friends beneath it never fall out.

May the doctor never earn a pound out of you.

May your glass be ever full.

May the sons of your daughters smile up in your face.

May your soul already be in Heaven a half hour before the devil knows you're dead.

May the grass on the road to Hell grow long for want of us.

May your home always be too small to hold all your friends.

Bless your little Irish heart and every other Irish part.

May the luck of the Irish be with you.

If God sends you down a stony path, may he give you strong shoes.

May I see you in Heaven.

May you live to be one hundred years with one extra year to repent.

May you get all your wishes but one, so that you will always have something to strive for.

May the horns of your cattle always touch heather.

May you live and wear it.

May the strength of three be in your journey.

May God not weaken your hand.

May the wind at your back always be your own.

May the face of every good news and the back of every bad news be towards us.

May the saddest day of your future be no worse than the happiest day of your past.

May your voice be above every voice.

One hundred thousand welcomes!

Here's to those who've seen us at our best and seen us at our worst and can't tell the difference.

May our sons have rich fathers and beautiful mothers.

CHAPTER TWO

Drinking, Humorous, and Specialty Toasts

The abiding Irish experience would be incomplete without toasts grounded in rich and sometimes biting humor. And, too, there are special drinking toasts for any and all occasions—some quite serious and others very funny.

Drinking Toasts

May the winds of fortune sail you,
May you sail a gentle sea,
May it always be the other guy
Who says, "This drink's on me."

May you never lie, steal, cheat, or drink.
But if you must lie,
Lie in each other's arms.
If you must steal,
Steal kisses.
If you must cheat,
Cheat death.
And if you must drink,
Drink with us, your friends.

Irish Curses, Blessings, and Toasts

My friends are the best friends,
Loyal, willing, and able.
Now let's get to drinking!
All glasses off the table!

That the tap may be open when it rusts!

Here's to a long life and a merry one,
A quick death and an easy one,
A pretty girl and an honest one,
A cold pint and another one.

Here's to a temperance supper
With water in glasses tall,
And coffee and tea to end with,
And me not there at all!

When money's tight and hard to get,
And your horse is also-ran,
When all you have is a heap of debt,
A pint of plain is your only man.

I drink to your health when I'm with you,
I drink to your health when I'm alone,
I drink to your health so often,
I'm starting to worry about my own!

May you always have
A clean shirt,
A clear conscience,
And enough coins in your pocket
    to buy a pint!

I have known many,
Liked not a few,
Loved only one,
I drink to you.

There are several good reasons for drinking
And one has just entered my head.
If a man can't drink when he's living,
Then how the heck can he drink when he's dead.

When we drink, we get drunk.
When we get drunk, we fall asleep.
When we fall asleep, we commit no sin.
When we commit no sin, we go to Heaven.
So, let's all get drunk, and go to Heaven!

In all this world, why I do think
There are five reasons why we drink:
Good friends,
Good wine,
Lest we be dry,
And any other reason why.

Be one who drinks the finest of ales
Every day and without fail.
Even when you have drank enough,
Remember that ale is wonderful stuff.

For every wound, a balm.
For every sorrow, cheer.
For every storm, a calm.
For every thirst, a beer.

In Heaven there is no beer,
That's why we drink ours here.

Here's a toast to the roast that good fellowship lends
With the sparkle of beer and wine.
May its sentiment always be deeper, my friends,
Than the foam at the top of the stein.

Life, alas, is very drear.
Up with the glass,
Down with the beer!

Here's to living single and drinking double!

Here's to being single, drinking double, and seeing
triple!

Four blessings upon you:
Older whiskey,
Younger women,
Faster horses,
More money.

We drink to your coffin.
May it be built from the wood
Of a hundred-year-old oak tree
That I shall plant tomorrow.

A bird with one wing can't fly.

It is better to spend money
    like there's no tomorrow
Than to spend tonight like
    there's no money!

The health of the salmon and of the trout
That swim back and forward near the Bull's Mouth.
Don't ask for saucepan, jug, or mug,
Down the hatch—drink it up!
May you be across Heaven's threshold
Before the old boy knows your dead.

Humorous Toasts

May those who love us, love us,
And those who don't love us,
May God turn their hearts,
And if he can't turn their hearts,
May he turn their ankles
So we will know them by their limping.

Here's to me,
And here's to you,
And here's to love and laughter.
I'll be true as long as you.
And not one moment after.

Here's to women's kisses,
And to whiskey, amber clear.
Not as sweet as a woman's kiss,
But a darn sight more sincere!

As you slide down the banisters of life,
May the splinters never point the wrong way.

May the light always find you on a dreary day,
When you need to be home, may you find your way.
May you always have courage to take a chance
And never find frogs in your underpants.

May your troubles be as few and as far apart as my
   Grandmother's teeth.

May your doctor never earn a dollar out of you
And may your heart never give out.
May the ten toes of your feet steer you clear of all
   misfortune,
And before you're much older,
May you hear much better toasts than this.

Here's to the wine we love to drink,
And the food we like to eat.
Here's to our wives and sweethearts,
Let's pray they never meet.
Here's champagne for our real friends,
And real pain for our sham friends.
And when this life is over,
May all of us find peace.

May you work like you don't need the money,
Love like you've never been hurt,
Dance like no one is watching,
Screw like it's being filmed,
And drink like a true Irishman.

May the enemies of Ireland never eat bread nor
    drink whiskey,
But be afflicted with itching without the benefit of
    scratching.

May the devil make a ladder of your backbone
While he is picking apples in the garden of Hell.

May your feet never sweat,
Your neighbor give you ne're a treat.
When flowers bloom, I hope you'll not sneeze,
And may you always have someone to squeeze!

Here's to Eve the mother of us all,
And here's to Adam
Who was Johnny on the spot
When the leaf began to fall.

May the good Lord
Take a liking to you,
But not too soon!

To live above with the saints we love,
Ah, that is the purest glory.
To live below with the saints we know,
Ah, that is another story!

May you fly straight to Heaven,
But if you go to Hades,
May Lethe run with Guinness!

Here's to the bull that roams through the wood,
And does all the heifers so very much good.
For if it was nay for him and his little red rod,
There'd be none of here could eat steak by God.

Here's to staying positive and testing negative.

May we get what we want, but never what we
      deserve.

Here's to you as good as you are,
And here's to me as bad as I am.
As good as you are and as bad as I am,
I'm as good as you are
As bad as I am!

Irish Curses, Blessings, and Toasts

Blessings for Special People, Places, and Occasions

Advent

On this first Sunday of Advent,
May the coming light that is our Lord
Fill you and yours with joy and peace.
During the coming Christmas season
May you be blessed
With the spirit of the season,
Which is peace,
The gladness of the season,
Which is hope,
And the heart of the season,
Which is love.

Bachelor Party

May you have nicer legs than yours under the table
   before the new spuds are up.

Back to School

May the patron saints of scholars and academics:
Brigid of Ireland, Catherine of Alexandria, Nicholas
   of Myra, and Thomas Aquinas
Ask the Father of all knowledge to bless students
   with a love of learning
And their teachers with wisdom and understanding.

Christening and Newborn Baby

May you always walk in sunshine,
May you never want for more,
May Irish angels rest their wings
Beside your nursery door.
And for the proud parents,
May God grant you
A wee bit of Heaven
To cradle in your arms,
A sweet bonny baby
To hold close to your heart.
A newborn babe
Brings light to the house,
Warmth to the hearth,
And joy to the soul.
For wealth is family,
Family is wealth.

A Gaelic Christening Blessing

Dearest Father in Heaven,
Bless this child and bless this day
Of new beginnings.
Smile upon this child
And surround this child, Lord,
With the soft mantle of your love.
Teach this child to follow in your footsteps,
And to live life in the ways of
Love, faith, hope, and charity.

Christmas

May peace and plenty be the first,
To lift the latch to your door.
And happiness be guided to your home,
By the candle of Christmas.

The magic of Christmas lingers on
Though childhood days have passed
Upon the common round of life
A Holy Spell is cast.

Here's to holly and ivy hanging up,
And to something wet in every cup.

Nollaig shona duit!
Happy Christmas!

Nollaig faoi shéan is faoi shonas duit.
A prosperous and happy Christmas to you.

Eulogy

Until we meet again,
May God hold you
In the palm of His hand.

Grieve not nor speak of me with tears,
But laugh and talk of me
As though I were beside you.
I loved you so,
'Twas heaven here with you.

Don't grieve for me
For now I'm free,
I follow the plan God laid for me.
I saw His face,
I heard His call,
I took His hand
And left it all.
I could not stay another day,
To love, to laugh, to work, or play.
Tasks left undone must stay that way,
And if my parting has left a void,

Then fill it with remembered joy.
A friendship shared, a laugh, a kiss,
Ah yes, these things I, too, shall miss.
My life's been full, I've savored much:
Good times, good friends, a loved one's touch.
Perhaps my time seemed all too brief,
Don't shorten yours with undue grief.
Be not burdened with tears of sorrow,
Enjoy the sunshine of the morrow.

Father's Day

May God bless all the dads
On this their special day.
Keep them safe,
Keep them whole,
And keep them from harm's way.

Feast of St. Francis

God bless the cow that gives us milk,
God bless the lamb that gives us wool,
God bless the hen that gives us eggs,
God bless the pig that pays the rent,
God bless the horse that we may ride,
God bless the cat that catches mice,
God bless the dog that herds the sheep,
God bless the geese for our feather beds,
God bless the lark for her morning song,
God bless the swan upon the pond,
God bless all friends of fur and feather
And St. Francis protect them in all weather.

Friendship

Miles and miles of Irish smiles
For golden happy hours,
Shamrocks at your doorway
For luck and laughter too,
And a host of friends that never ends
Each day your whole life through.

Here's to the nights we'll never remember with the
friends we'll never forget.

Grace

Bless us, O God.
Bless our food and our drink.
Since you redeemed us so dearly
And delivered us from evil,
As you gave us a share in this food
So may you give us a share in eternal life.

May this food restore our strength,
Giving new energy to tired limbs,
And new thoughts to weary minds.
May this drink restore our souls,
Giving new vision to dry spirits,
And new warmth to cold hearts.
And once nourished and refreshed,
May we give thanks to Him who
Gives us all and makes us blessed.

God willing, may our tea
Be steeped in serenity,
Sweetened by sharing,
And surrounded by the
Warmth of your love.

Hearth and Home

God bless the corners of this house
And be the lintel blessed.
Bless the hearth, the table too,
And bless each place of rest.
Bless each door that opens wide
To stranger, kith, and kin.
Bless each shining windowpane
That lets the sunshine in.
Bless the rooftree up above.
Bless every solid wall.
The peace of man, the peace of love,
The peace of God on all.

Holy Week

May God in His infinite mercy
Grant you and yours a journey
Of renewal and hope,
A time of prayer and reflection,
And joyful anticipation
Of our Lord's resurrection.

In Memory Of

To absent friends.

Ireland, Erin's Green Isle

Ireland,
It's the one place on earth
That Heaven has kissed
With melody, mirth, meadow, and mist.

Hills as green as emeralds
Cover the countryside.
Lakes as blue as sapphires
Are Ireland's special pride.
And rivers that shine like silver
Make Ireland look so fair.
But the friendliness of her people
Is the richest treasure there.

How sweetly lies old Ireland
Emerald green beyond the foam,
Awakening sweet memories,
Calling the heart back home.

Green are the hills of Ireland
And green they will always stay.
Warm are the blessing wished for you
And they'll always be that way.

As lovely as Erin's rolling hills,
Fair as its lakes and streams,
Joyful as its laughter,
Bright as all its dreams,
Lucky as its people,
Happy as its leprechauns too,
May that be how each and every day
Will always be for you.

Have you ever been to Ireland
With its rolling hills so green?
Sure 'n it's the fairest land
That ever has been seen.
And those green hills of Ireland
May be very far away,
But they're close to every Irish heart
No matter what the day.

There are millions of shamrocks
On Erin's green isle,
Thousands of Irishmen
Wearing a smile,
Hundreds of Irish lakes
Sparkling blue,
But only one wonderful
Person like you.

Here's to dear old Erin
That lovely Emerald Isle.
Here's to every colleen
And every colleen's smile.
Here's to Irish laughter
And the Little People too.
Here's to dear old Erin,
But most of all
Here's to you!

Take all the many shamrocks
Growin' green on Erin's Isle.
Take all the lilting Irish tunes
And every Irish smile.
Just add them all together
And you'll find they're quite a few.
But surely not as many
As my special thoughts of you.

Health and a long life to you,
Land without rent to you,
A child every year to you,
And if you can't go to Heaven,
May you at least die in Ireland.

Here's to the land of the shamrock so green,
Here's to each lad and his darlin' colleen,
Here's to the ones we love dearest and most.
May God bless old Ireland,
That's this Irishman's toast!

Health and long life to you,
Land without rent to you,
The partner of your heart to you,
And when you die,
May your bones rest in Ireland!

It would take more lucky shamrocks
Than Ireland ever grew
To bring the luck and gladness
That I'm always wishing you.

Lent

Merciful God, you called us forth
From the dust of the earth.
You claimed us for Christ
In the waters of baptism.
Look upon us as we enter these Forty Days
Bearing the mark of ashes,
And bless our journey through the desert of Lent
To the font of rebirth.
May our fasting be hunger for justice,
Our alms, a making of peace,
Our prayer, the chant of humble and
    grateful hearts.
All that we do and pray is
In the name of Jesus.
For in His cross you proclaim
Your love for ever and ever.

Mother

Of all of God's blessings
The love of an Irish mother
Is constant and pure
And unlike any other.
May angels of God
Bring her blessings unbounded
As with His love and her
children's, today, she's surrounded.

God made a wonderful mother,
A mother who never grows old.
He made her smile of the sunshine,
And He molded her heart of pure gold.
In her eyes He placed bright shining stars,
In her cheeks, fair roses you see.
God made a wonderful mother,
And He gave that dear mother to me.

Irish Curses, Blessings, and Toasts

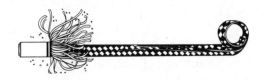

New Year

In the New Year,
May your right hand always
Be stretched out in friendship
And never in want.

May the New Year bring
The warmth of home and hearth to you,
The cheer and goodwill of friends to you,
The hope of a childlike heart to you,
The joy of a thousand angels to you,
The love of the Son and God's peace to you.

Go mbeire muid beo ar an am seo arís.
May we be alive at this time next year.

Athbhliain faoi mhaise duit!
A prosperous New Year!

Saint Patrick's Day

Saint Patrick was a gentleman
Who through strategy and stealth,
Drove all the snakes from Ireland.
Here's a toasting to his health,
But not too many toastings
Lest you lose yourself and then
Forget the good Saint Patrick
And see all those snakes again.

Beannachtam na Feile Padraig!
Happy St. Patrick's Day!

Summertime

May the sun shine bright on your joyous days
And the rain refresh you through peaceful nights.
May summer show you God's wondrous ways
And prepare you for Heaven's great delights.

Sympathy

May you see God's light on the path ahead
When the road you walk is dark.
May you always hear,
Even in your hour of sorrow,
The gentle singing of the lark.
When times are hard,
May hardness never turn your heart to stone.
May you always remember
When the shadows fall,
You do not walk alone.

Wedding

Sliocht sleachta ar shliocht bhur sleachta.
May there be a generation of children on
    the children of your children.

Here's an Irish toast to your wedding:
May the roof over your heads be as well thatched
As those inside are well matched.

'Til death comes to part us asunder.

Wedding Prayer

By the power that Christ brought from Heaven,
Mayst thou love me.
As the sun follows its course,
Mayst thou follow me.
As light to the eye,
As bread to the hungry,
As joy to the heart,
May thy presence be with me,
Oh one that I love.

Irish Curses, Blessings, and Toasts

CHAPTER THREE

Saint Patrick, Saint Brigid, and Special Prayers

There are many Irish blessings and prayers that cite Ireland's patron saints: Patrick and Brigid. Often they are asked to intercede on behalf of someone. Sometimes their services are enlisted to watch over and protect someone or something.

Saint Patrick

Saint Patrick's Prayer
This day I call to me:
God's strength to direct me,
God's power to sustain me,
God's wisdom to guide me,
God's vision to light me,
God's ear to my hearing,
God's word to my speaking,
God's hand to uphold me,
God's pathway before me,
God's shield to protect me,
God's legions to save me.

May good Saint Patrick bless you
And keep you in his care.
And may Our Lord be near you
To answer every prayer.

May good Saint Patrick bring you
Each blessing that endures.
And may his spirit evermore
Abide with you and yours.

As he brought new faith to Ireland
So may he bring to you,
A touch of Irish happiness
In everything you do.
And like the good Saint Patrick,
May your home and life be blessed
With all God's special favors
That make you happiest.

May Saint Patrick guard you wherever you go,
And guide you in whatever you do,
And may his loving protection be a blessing to you
    always.

May the Irish hills caress you,
May her lakes and rivers bless you,
May the luck of the Irish enfold you,
And may the blessings of Saint Patrick behold you.

Irish Curses, Blessings, and Toasts

May Saint Patrick intercede on your behalf
And God be beside you when you walk,
In your voice when you talk,
In your eyes when you see,
In your ears when you hear,
In your heart when you pray,
In your mind when you think,
And in your hands when you touch.
In every sense may it be
That God is with you eternally.

A happy, generous nature,
A friendly spirit too,
These are the gifts Saint Patrick
Has surely given you.
And may every day to come
Bring a generous part
Of all the happy things in life
That keep joy in your heart.

In the name of dear Saint Patrick
This brings a loving prayer.
May you forever be within
God's tender loving care.
May your heart be filled with happiness,
Your home be filled with laughter
And may the Holy Trinity
Bless your life forever after.

May the good Saint Patrick love you
And ask Our Lord to bless
You and all your dear ones
With wealth and happiness.

May your days be very happy,
May your life be free from cares,
May Saint Patrick ask our Blessed Lord
To answer all your prayers.

May our blessed good Saint Patrick
Whom we all so dearly love
Intercede and bring you
Many blessings from above.

May all the giant hearts be tall as day,
May all your winter nights be warm as May,
May the love and protection Saint Patrick can give
Be yours in abundance as long as you live.

As sure as the shamrocks are growing
In the land which the Irish all love.
As sure as the lakes of Killarney
Reflect the blue heavens above.
As sure as the warmhearted Irish
All pay honor to Saint Patrick too,
I'm wishing you "top o' the morning"
And happiness, always, for you.

May all the joy that echoes through
A happy Irish song,
And all the luck the shamrock brings,
Be yours the whole year long.
May you have blessings, pleasures, friends,
To gladden all life's way.
And may Saint Patrick smile on you
Today and every day.

Here's to the Land of the Shamrock
Where Irish hearts are true.
Here's to our blessed Saint Patrick
But most of all, here's to you.

There's a dear little plant that grows in our isle,
'Twas Saint Patrick himself sure that set it.
And the sun on his labor with pleasure did smile
And a tear from his eye oft-times wet it.
It grows through the bog, through the brake,
    through the mireland,
And they call it the dear little Shamrock of Ireland.

May your hope be:
As determined as the river racing by,
As soft as the cry of the mourning dove,
As sweet and subtle as a lover's sigh,
As resolute as the sun rising each day,
As certain as the return each year of spring.
May it break through the darkling clouds
And confirm you against every evil thing.
May Jesus and Mary and Patrick and Brigid
Strengthen your faith and hope and love,
And may God bless you,
Father, Son, and Holy Spirit.

Saint Patrick's Breastplate

I arise today
Through a mighty strength, the invocation of the
    Trinity,
Through belief in the Threeness,
Through confession of the Oneness
Of the Creator of creation.
I arise today
Through the strength of Christ's birth with
    His baptism,
Through the strength of His crucifixion with
    His burial,
Through the strength of His resurrection with
    His ascension,
Through the strength of His descent for the
    judgment of doom.
I arise today
Through the strength of the love of cherubim,
In the obedience of angels,
In the service of archangels,
In the hope of resurrection to meet with reward,
In the prayers of patriarchs,

In the predictions of prophets,
In the preaching of apostles,
In the faith of confessors,
In the innocence of holy virgins,
In the deeds of righteous men.
I arise today, through
The strength of Heaven,
The light of the sun,
The radiance of the moon,
The splendor of fire,

The speed of lightning,
The swiftness of wind,
The depth of the sea,
The stability of the earth,
The firmness of rock.
I arise today, through
God's strength to pilot me,
God's might to uphold me,
God's wisdom to guide me,
God's eye to look before me,

God's ear to hear me,
God's word to speak for me,
God's hand to guard me,
God's shield to protect me,
God's host to save me
From snares of devils,
From temptation of vices,
From everyone who shall wish me ill,
Afar and near.
I summon today
All these powers between me and those evils,
Against every cruel and merciless power
That may oppose my body and soul,
Against incantations of false prophets,
Against black laws of pagandom,
Against false laws of heretics,
Against craft of idolatry,
Against spells of witches and smiths and wizards,
Against every knowledge that corrupts man's body
and soul.

Christ to shield me today
Against poison, against burning,
Against drowning, against wounding,
So that there may come to me an abundance of
    reward.
Christ with me,
Christ before me,
Christ behind me,
Christ in me,
Christ beneath me,
Christ above me,
Christ on my right,
Christ on my left,
Christ when I lie down,
Christ when I sit down,
Christ when I arise,
Christ in the heart of every man who thinks of me,
Christ in the mouth of everyone who speaks of me,
Christ in every eye that sees me,
Christ in every ear that hears me.

Saint Brigid of Kildare

Saint Brigid's Blessing

Through her holy intercession
With our Father in Heaven,
May Saint Brigid bless
You and make you
Generous in your giving,
Pleasant in your greeting,
Honest in your speaking,
Loyal in your loving,
Clear in your thinking,
Strong in your working,
And joyful in your living.
And when it's time
For your homecoming,
May there be peace in
Your passing and a warm
Welcome in Heaven.

Saint Brigid House Blessing

May Brigid bless the house where you dwell,
Every fireside door and every wall,
Every heart that beats beneath its róof,
Every hand that toils to bring it joy,
Every foot that walks its portals through.
May Brigid bless the house that shelters you.

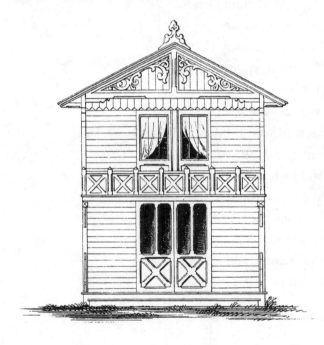

Irish Curses, Blessings, and Toasts

Saint Brigid Safe Travel Blessing

O Brigid, bless our road,
That calamity may not overtake us as we travel.
O veiled one from the laden Liffey,
May we reach home safely by your intercession.

May there be a fox on your fishing hook
And a hare on your bait.
And may you kill no fish
Until Saint Brigid's Day (February 1st).

Special Religious Blessings

May the God of the misty dawn waken you,
May the God of the rising sun stir you up,
May the God of morning sky send you on your way,
May the God of noonday stillness renew your
    strength,
May the God of afternoon bring you home,
May the God of sunset delight your eye,
May the God of twilight calm your nerves,
And the God of dusk bring you peace.
And may God bless you:
The Rising and the Setting Sun,
The Alpha and the Omega,
The Beginning and the End,
Father, Son, and Holy Spirit.

May each day have its own wonder and rebirth,
Its molding of new life from unwilling clay,
Its springing in surprise from reluctant earth,
Its hint of victory on final Judgment Day.
And may the God of daily resurrections bless you,
Father, Son, and Holy Spirit.

May the Good Shepherd
Protect you in
Ups and downs,
Ins and outs,
Bounds and rebounds,
Highs and lows,
Comings and goings,
Heat and cold,
Darkness and light,
Joy and sorrow,
Good times and bad times,
Daytimes and nighttimes,
Short times and long times,
Old times and new times.
May He be with you
At home and abroad,

On the road and at rest,
In storm and flood,
In drought and desert,
In peace and conflict,
In doubt and assurance,
In sickness and health,
In pain and triumph.
May the Good Shepherd walk
With you always
Until it is time to return home.
And may God bless you,
Father, Son, and Holy Spirit.

May you treasure wisely this jeweled, gilded time
And cherish each day as an extra grace
Whose heedless loss would be a tragic crime.
In today's tasks may you find God's tender face,
May you know that to miss love's smallest chance
Is a lost opportunity, a senseless waste.
May you see need in every anxious glance,
May you sort out of the dull and commonplace
An invitation to God's merry, manic dance.
And may the Lord of the dance bless you

As he invites you to the dance of the hallowed
    present,
Father, Son, and Holy Spirit. Amen.

May the morning sun stir you out of bed,
May the winter winds move you on the road,
May the rains of March renew your strength,
May the flowers of spring captivate your sight,
May summer heat inflame your zeal,
May autumn color stimulate your dreams,

May the silver moon make you wiser yet,
May you never be with yourself content,
May Jesus and Mary keep you young,
Full of life and laughter and love.
And may the God of challenge and adventure
Bless you and keep you always,
Father, Son, and Holy Spirit.

Deep peace of the running waves to you,
Deep peace of the flowing air to you,
Deep peace of the smiling stars to you,
Deep peace of the quiet earth to you,
Deep peace of the watching shepherds to you,
Deep peace of the Son of Peace to you.

Special Prayers

May the power of God this day enable me,
The nakedness of God disarm me,
The beauty of God silence me,
The justice of God give me voice,
The integrity of God hold me,
The desire of God move me,
The fear of God expose me to the truth,
The breath of God give me abundant life.

Circle me Lord,
Keep protection near,
And danger afar.
Circle me Lord,
Keep hope within,
Keep doubt without.
Circle me Lord,
Keep light near,
And darkness afar.
Circle me Lord,
Keep peace within,
Keep evil out.

You've blessed me with friends
And laughter and fun,
With rain that's as soft
As the light from the sun.
You've blessed me with stars
To brighten each night.
You've given me help
To know wrong from right.
You've given me so much.
Please Lord, give me too
A heart that is always
Grateful to you.

Bless us O Lord, You who are
The peace of all things calm,
The place to hide from harm,
The light that shines in dark,
The heart's eternal spark,
The door that's open wide
Welcoming all to come inside.
We ask this blessing
God be willing.

Funeral Prayer

Death is nothing at all.
It does not count.
I have only slipped away into the next room.
Everything remains as it was.
The old life that we lived so fondly together
Is untouched, unchanged.
Whatever we were to each other, that we are still.
Call me by the old familiar name.
Speak of me in the easy way which you always
    used.
Put no sorrow in your tone.
Laugh as we always laughed at the little jokes
That we enjoyed together.
Play, smile, think of me, pray for me.
Let my name be ever the household word
That it always was.

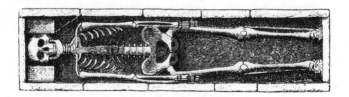

Let it be spoken without effort.
Life means all that it ever meant.
It is the same as it ever was.
There is unbroken continuity.
Why should I be out of mind
Because I am out of sight?
I am but waiting for you, for an interval,
Somewhere very near, just around the corner.
All is well. Nothing is hurt. Nothing is lost.
One brief moment and all will be as it was before.
How we shall laugh at the trouble of parting,
When we meet again.

Prayer of Consolation

I pray that you will have the blessing of
    being consoled.
May you know in your soul that there is no need
    to be afraid.
When your time comes, may you be given every
    blessing and shelter that you need.
May there be a beautiful welcome for you in the
    home that you are going to.
You are not going somewhere strange.
You are going back to the home that you never left.
May you have a wonderful urgency to live your life
    to the full.
May you live compassionately and creatively and
    transfigure everything that is negative within
    you and about you.
When you come to die, may it be after a long life.
May you be peaceful and happy and in the presence
    of those who really care for you.
May your going be sheltered and your welcome
    assured.
May your soul smile in the embrace of your *anam
    cara* (soul friend).

Prayer for Good Humor
by Saint Thomas More

Grant me, O Lord, good digestion, and also some-
    thing to digest.
Grant me a healthy body, and the necessary good
    humor to maintain it.
Grant me a simple soul that knows to treasure all
    that is good
And that doesn't frighten easily at the sight of evil,
But rather finds the means to put things back in
    their place.
Give me a soul that knows not boredom, grum-
    blings, sighs, and laments,
Nor excess of stress, because of that obstructing
    thing called "I."
Grant me, O Lord, a sense of good humor.
Allow me the grace to be able to take a joke to dis-
    cover in life a bit of joy,
And to be able to share it with others.

CHAPTER FOUR

Curses

*When the circumstances warrant, the singular Irish
gift for words can turn lethal. To wish enemies ill, the
Irish have a wealth of curses from which to choose.
Some of them are terse and get right to the point,
while others are a bit more labyrinthine.*

May the enemies of Ireland never eat bread nor drink whiskey, but be afflicted with itching without the benefit of scratching.

May you be afflicted with the itch and have no nails to scratch with.

The curse of the crows on you.

The raven's curse on you.

May you marry a wench that blows wind like a stone from a sling.

May your obituary be written in weasel's piss.

Go to the dickens.

A cold day on you.

In hell may you be because of your sins.

Bad luck on him.

May your trouble be in your throat.

May it do him no good only sorrow.

May he never have a day's luck.

May your choking come on you.

May a stitch or convulsion strike you.

A poisonous pain in you.

Death and smothering on you.

Dysentery on you.

May he fester in his grave.

A death without a priest to him in a town without a clergyman.

May you not see the cuckoo nor the corncrake.

My curse on you and ruin to you
You lying, thieving rascal.

A fox on your fishing hook.

The curse of Cromwell on you.

A mountain landslide down upon you.

May the mice come in waves as his company
and the rats from the kiln give him the
pursuit.

The curse of widows and orphans on you.

A high windy gallows to him.

A red stone in your throat.

May every day of it be wet for ye.

May you have no good luck and I can't recant the
curse.

May you all go to hell and not have a drop of porter to quench your eternal thirst.

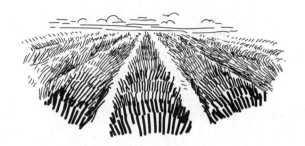

May there never be enough of your people to make a half-set. (A set is a traditional dance with eight people; a half-set is with four people.)

If your crop is tall, may your meitheal be small. (A meitheal was a group of friends and neighbors who would cooperate with one another at harvest time. The help of others was essential in getting the work done.)

Blast you to hell!

May you never have a hearth to call your own.

May the gates of paradise never open to you.

That you may scratch a beggarman's back one day.

May you lose everything you have.

May there be guinea-fowl crying (considered bad luck) at your child's birth.

Bad cess to you! (Cess is an Irish slang word for luck.)

May you marry in haste and repent at leisure.

May you have the runs on your wedding night.

May you be eaten by an awful itch!

To hell with you!

May all the goats in Gorey chase you to hell. (Gorey is a small town in County Wexford.)

Pissmires and spiders be in your marriage bed. (Pissmires are ants.)

Curse of the seven snotty orphans on you.

May you find the bees but miss the honey.

That you may be a load for four before
the year is out. (It typically required four
people to carry a coffin.)

The curse of his weapons upon him.

May the curse of Mary Malone and her nine blind
illegitimate children chase you so far over the Hills
of Damnation that the Lord himself can't find you
with a telescope.

May you leave without returning.

May you melt off the earth like snow off a ditch.

May you be mangled.

May your spuds be like rosary-beads on the stalk.

May you melt off the earth like snow off the ditch.

The Devil

May the cat eat you and may
the devil eat the cat.
Your soul to the devil!

May the devil make a fool of you.

I give you to the devil.

May the devil cut the head off you and make a
day's work of your neck.

May the devil take him by the heels and shake him.

May the devil tear you.

The devil mend you!

I give you to the devil.

May the devil damn you to the stone of dirges
Or to the well of ashes seven miles below hell.
And may the devil break your bones
And all my calamity and harm and misfortune
For a year on you.

May the devil swallow
him sideways.

May the devil take your
last shilling!

God and Prayer

May God weaken you.

Curse of God on you.

God damn your soul to hell.

Let it not be long till you die despite the Son of God.

I pray for sorrow on the house.

The curse of Jesus on you.

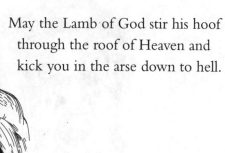

May the Lamb of God stir his hoof through the roof of Heaven and kick you in the arse down to hell.

From "Nell Flaherty's Drake"

Bad luck to the robber be he drunk or sober
That murdered Nell Flaherty's beautiful drake.
May his spade never dig, may his sow never pig,
May each hair in his wig be well trashed with
    the flail.
May his door never latch, may his roof have
    no thatch,
May his turkeys not hatch, may the rats eat his meal,
May every old fairy from Cork to Dun Laoghaire
Dip him snug and airy in river or lake
That the eel and the trout they may dine on
    the snout
Of the monster that murdered Nell Flaherty's drake.
May his pig never grunt, may his cat never hunt,
May a ghost ever haunt him the dead of the night,
May his hens never lay, may his horse never neigh,
May his coat fly away like an old paper kite,
That the flies and the fleas may the wretch ever
    tease,
May the piercin' March breeze make
    him shiver and shake

May a lump of the stick raise the bumps fast and
    quick
On the monster that murdered Nell Flaherty's
    drake.

Lord, confound this surly sister,
Blight her brow with blotch and blister,
Cramp her larynx, lung, and liver,
In her guts a galling give her.

                       —*John Millington Synge*

No butter be on your milk
Nor on your ducks a web.
May your cow be flayed
And may the flame be bigger and wider
Which will go through your soul
Than the Connemara mountains,
If they were on fire.

May you have a little skillet,
May you have little in it,
May you have to break it,
To find the little bit in it.

CHAPTER FIVE

Proverbs and Sayings

Every ethnicity and culture has its very own proverbs and sayings. But the Irish—perhaps more than any other—have maxims and witty insights that touch upon every aspect of humanity and human nature. From beginnings to endings, the Irish have left no stone unturned.

Age and Experience

Age is a very high price to pay for maturity.

As the old cock crows, the young cock learns.

Though wisdom is good in the beginning, it is better at the end.

Many a ragged colt made a noble horse.

The older the fiddle the sweeter the tune.

Age is honorable and youth is noble.

The old person is a child twice.

Two good things: a young man courting, an old man smoking. Two bad things: an old man courting, a young man smoking.

Do not resent growing old. Many are not given the privilege.

Beautiful young people are acts of nature, but beautiful old people are works of art.

An old broom knows the dirty corners best.

It's hard to teach an old dog to dance.

An old man's child is hard to rear.

Young people don't know what old age is, and old people forget what youth was.

Beginnings

When a twig grows hard it is difficult to twist it. Every beginning is weak.

Calendar and Weather

A misty winter brings a pleasant spring; a pleasant
    winter a misty spring.

A wet and windy May fills the barn with corn and
    hay.

Better April showers than the breadth of the ocean
    in gold.
Many a sudden change takes place on a spring day.

If Candlemas (February 2nd) is wet or foul, half the
    winter has gone at Yule. If Candlemas is fine
    and fair, half the winter is to come and more.

Life goes on as quickly as if it had wings, and each
    Christmas places another year on your shoulders.

Hearing crickets on Christmas is a good omen for
    the new year.

Choices

Don't change your horse when you are about to cross a river.

It is better to be a coward for a minute than dead for the rest of your life.

Five frogs are sitting on a log. Four decide to jump off. How many are left? Answer: five.
Why? Because there's a difference between deciding and doing.

A look in front is better than two behind.

Courage

The brave man never loses.

If you're the only one that knows you're afraid,
   you're brave.

Fortune favors the brave.

Every hound is brave on his own dunghill.

Death

Death is the poor man's best physician.

Nobody knows where his sod of death is.

Death does not take a bribe.

There is hope from the sea, but none from the grave.

A man at sea may return, but not the man in the
   churchyard.

Drinking

A drink precedes a story.

Good as drink is, it ends in thirst.

What butter or whiskey does not cure cannot be
cured.

There's little profit from being always drunk.

When the liquor was gone, the fun was gone.

Man's way to God is with beer in hand.

Drunkenness will not protect a secret.

A mouth of a perfectly happy man is filled
with beer.

Beer drinkin' don't do half the harm of love makin'.

Women do not drink liquor, but it disappears when
 they are present.

It is sweet to drink but bitter to pay for.

Thirst is a shameless disease.

Morning is the time to pity the sober. The way
 they're feeling then is the best they're going to
 feel all day.

Thirst is the end of drinking and sorrow is the end
 of drunkenness.

Three diseases without shame: love, itch, and thirst.

In Heaven there is no beer, that is why we drink it
 here.

Wine divulges truth.

Thirst is a shameless disease, so here's to a shameful
 cure.

Daylight comes through the drunkard's roof the
  fastest.

I'll have what the man on the floor's having!

I've always believed that paradise will have my
  favorite beer on tap.

No animal ever invented anything as bad as drunkenness or as good as drink.

Drunk is feeling sophisticated when you can't say it.

The best beer is where priests go to drink.

Beer makes you feel the way you ought to feel
  without beer.

History flows forward on rivers of beer.

Those who drink to forget, please pay in advance.

Man, being reasonable, must get drunk. The best of life is but intoxication.

Before you call for one for the road be sure you know the road.

The truth comes out when the spirit goes in.

It's the first drop that destroys you. There's no harm at all in the last.

He'd step over ten naked women to get at a pint.

A narrow neck keeps the bottle from being emptied in one swig.

Family

As the big hound is, so will the pup be.

What the child sees is what the child does.

You've got to do your own growing, no matter
how tall your father was.

A son is a son till he takes him a wife. A daughter is
a daughter all of her life.

No son is as good as his father in his sister's eyes. No
father is as good as his son in his mother's eyes.

Every mother thinks it is on her own child the sun
rises.

Blood is thicker than water and easier seen.

Praise and scold in equal measure, if your family
you treasure.

The family that has no skeleton in a cupboard has
buried it instead.

Fools

A fool's money is not long in his pocket.

A fool's word is a thorn in the mud.

Don't give cherries to pigs or advice to fools.

Often a fool's son is a wise man.

There's no fool like an old fool.

He's fit to mind mice at a crossroads. (Said of pathetic fools.)

Pity him who makes his opinion a certainty.

Friends and Enemies

A friend's eye is a good mirror.

Who keeps his tongue keeps his friends.

No war is as bitter as a war between two friends, but it doesn't last long.

Tell me who your friends are and I'll tell you who you are.

The friend that can be bought is not worth buying.

Better fifty enemies outside the house than one inside it.

Both your friend and your enemy think you will never die.

The best way to get rid of your enemies is God's way, by loving them.

A constant guest is never welcome.

A nation's greatest enemy is the small minds of its
small people.

God and Faith

God's help is nearer than the door.

God helps him who helps himself.

The fear of God is the beginning of wisdom.

The mills of God grind slowly but they grind finely.

God moves slowly yet his grace comes.

He who loses money, loses much. He who loses a
friend, loses more. He who loses faith, loses all.

God made the back to suit the burden.

If there be a guest in your house and you conceal
 aught from him, 'tis not the guest who will be
 without, but Jesus, the Son of Mary.

God made time, but man made haste.

God prefers prayers to tears.

Get down on your knees and thank God you're still
 on your feet.

Hearth and Home

There is no fireside like your own fireside.

Empty and cold is the house without a woman.

There's trouble in every house and some in the
  street.

Irish Curses, Blessings, and Toasts

Honesty and Truth

The man that steals stacks thinks all the world thieves.

Even the truth may be bitter.

A lie travels farther than the truth.

Truth stands when everything else fails.

There are two tellings to every story.

Human Nature

The well-fed person doesn't understand the
    hungry one.

The losing horse blames the saddle.

You never miss the water until the well runs dry.

People live in one another's shelter.

Everyone is sociable until a cow invades his garden.

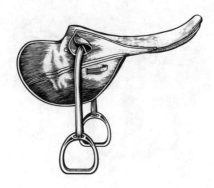

If he went to a wedding, he'd wait for the chris-
    tening. (Said of those who overstay their wel-
    comes.)

You might as well be whistling jigs to a milestone.
    (Said of those who are thick-headed.)

Instinct is stronger than upbringing.

'Tis only a stepmother would blame you. (Said of
    those who are blame-free.)

Quarrelsome dogs get dirty coats.

Everyone feels his own wound first.

A burnt child fears the fire.

Ireland and the Irish

Erin Go Bragh!
Ireland Forever!

Life's too short not to be Irish!

An Irishman carries his heart in his hand.

An Irishman is never at peace, except when he's
fighting.

The Irish forgive their great men when they are
safely buried.

Only Irish coffee provides all main essential food
groups: alcohol, caffeine, sugar, and fat.

What's the use of being Irish if the world doesn't break your heart?

God is good to the Irish, but no one else is—not even the Irish.

There are only three kinds of Irish men who can't understand women: young men, old men, and men of middle age.

The Irish do not want anyone to wish them well. They want everyone to wish their enemies ill.

If you're lucky enough to be Irish, then you're lucky enough.

God invented whiskey so the Irish wouldn't rule the world!

An Irishman is never drunk as long as he can hold on to one blade of grass and not fall off the face of the earth.

There are only two kinds of people in the world: the Irish and those who wish they were.

If wars were fought with words, Ireland would be ruling the world.

What is Irish diplomacy? It's the ability to tell a man to go to hell, so that he will look forward to making the trip.

You can't kiss an Irish girl unexpectedly. You can only kiss her sooner than she thought you would.

The devil invented Scotch whiskey to make the Irish poor.

A family of Irish birth will argue and fight, but let a shout come from without and see them all unite.

Have you heard about the Irish boomerang? It doesn't come back. It just sings sad songs about how much it wants to.

God then made man. The Italian for their beauty. The French for fine food. The Swedes for intelligence. The Jew for religion. And on and on until he looked at what He had created and said: "This is all very fine but no one is having fun. I guess I'll have to make me an Irishman."

Ireland is where strange tales begin and happy endings are possible.

Marry a mountain girl and you marry the whole mountain.

Love

It's easy to halve the potato
   where there's love.

Love cools quickly.

A man loves his sweetheart the most, his wife the
   best, but his mother the longest.

What is nearest the heart comes out.

What is nearest the heart is usually nearest the lips.

Death leaves a heartache no one can heal. Love
   leaves a memory no one can steal.

When the sight leaves the eye, love leaves the heart.

Beauty won't make the kettle boil.

Luck

The man who has luck in the morning has luck in
the afternoon.

A chance shot will not kill the devil.

A whistling woman and a crowing hen
will bring no luck to the house
they are in.

The lucky person has only to be born.

There is no luck except where there is discipline.

Manners and Civility

Better good manners than good looks.

What would you expect out of a pig but a grunt.
(Said of an uncouth person.)

Marriage

Two shorten the road.

The blanket is the warmer of being doubled.

Woe to him who does heed a good wife's counsel.

A man cannot grow rich without his wife's leave.

From the day you marry your heart will be in your
mouth and your hand in your pocket.

The only cure for love is marriage.

There are no trials till marriage.

If you want to be criticized, marry.

A bad wife takes advice from everyone but her husband.

If you want praise, die. If you want blame, marry.

Love is blind but marriage restores eyesight!

There is only one thing in the world better than a good wife—no wife.

Man is incomplete until he marries. After that, he is finished.

It's why women marry—the creatures, God bless them, are too shy to say no.

Marriages are all happy. It's having breakfast together that causes all the trouble.

Men and Women

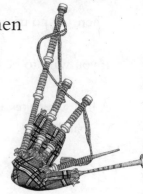

Men are like bagpipes—no sound
   comes from them until they
   are full.

A man without a blackthorn
   stick is a man without an
   expedient.

A man is a man when his woman is a woman.

A sea wind changes less often than the mind of a
   weak man.

A man's fame lasts longer than his life.

No man can prosper without his woman's leave.

Money, Wealth, and Debt

There is misfortune only where there is wealth.

A shamefaced man seldom acquires wealth.

If you want to know what God thinks of money,
    just look at who He gives it to.

He that is of the opinion that money will do
    everything may well be suspected
    of doing everything for money.

A heavy purse makes a light heart.

Forgetting a debt doesn't mean it's paid.

The full man does not understand the wants of the
    hungry.

Lack of resource has hanged many a person.

A little pleases a poor man.

A poor man never yet lost his property.

Enough and no waste is as good as a feast.

A dog owns nothing, yet is seldom dissatisfied.

He who marries money, marries a fool.

Need

Make necessity a virtue.

Necessity is the mother of invention.

Necessity knows no law.

There is no need like the lack of a friend.

Need teaches a plan.

Observation

The stars make no noise.

An empty sack won't stand.

The longest road out is the shortest road home.

It is a long road that has no turning.

On an unknown path every foot is slow.

When the belly is full, the bones like to stretch.

Dead men tell no tales but there's many a thing
learned in the wake-house.

We attract what we love and what we fear.

A hen is heavy when carried far.

The darkest hour is nearest the dawn.

A goose never voted for an early Christmas.

He who comes with a story to you brings two
   away from you.

In the long run, men hit only what they aim at.
   Therefore, they had better aim at something
   high.

A face without freckles is like a sky without stars.

When fire is applied to a stone, it cracks.

Firelight will not let you read fine stories, but it's
   warm, and you won't see the dust on the floor.

While a person is out, his food goes cold.

There's nothing so bad that it couldn't be worse.

They invented the three-day bank holiday weekend because you can't lump all the bad weather into just Saturday and Sunday.

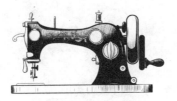

Occupation

There was often a bad cloth on a tailor and a bad shoe on a cobbler.

There is no woman more accustomed to bad shoes on her than the cobbler's wife.

One does not tire of a profitable occupation.

A long stitch, a lazy tailor.

Pain and Suffering

Even a small thorn causes festering.

Parenting

Be good to the child and he will come to you
tomorrow.

The trick the father has, the son has.

The apple does not fall far from the tree.

When the apple is ripe, it will fall.

A craftsman's son may grow up in ignorance of his
father's skills.

No man ever wore a cravat as nice as his own
child's arm around his neck.

No man ever wore a scarf as warm as his daughter's
arm around his neck.

Bricks and mortar make a house but the laughter of
children makes a home.

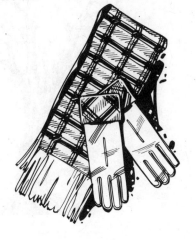

Patience

Patience is a poultice for all wounds.

Patience can conquer destiny.

Beware of the anger of a patient man.

There is not a tree higher in Heaven than the tree of patience.

Irish Curses, Blessings, and Toasts

Philosophy

A hole is more honorable than a patch.

A cabin with plenty of food is better than a hungry castle.

It is better to spend money like there's no tomorrow than to spend tonight like there's no money!

'Tis better to have fought and lost than never to have fought at all.

Take the world nice and easy and the world will take you the same.

The day will come when the cow will have use for her tail.

He who has water and peat on his own farm has the world his own way.

It's easy to have principles when you're rich. The important thing is to have principles when you're poor.

Praise the ripe field not the green corn.

Praise the ford when you have crossed it.

Be afraid and you will not meet danger.

Relationships

It is a lonely washing that has no man's shirt in it.

It's the last suitor that wins the maid.

Reputation and Honor

Better to be a man of character than a man of means.

He who gets a name for early rising can stay in bed until midday.

A man may live after losing his life but not after losing his honor.

It is more difficult to maintain honor than to become prosperous.

Better the trouble that follows death than the trouble that follows shame.

Remember even if you lose all, keep your good name, for if you lose that, you are worthless.

Silence

A silent mouth is sweet to hear.

A silent mouth is melodious.

A silent mouth never did any harm.

A wise head keeps a shut mouth.

It is the quiet pigs that eat the meal.

Quiet people are well able to look after themselves.

Say little but say it well.

When wrathful words arise, a closed mouth
is soothing.

Time

Time is a great storyteller.

A watched kettle never boils.

It takes time to build castles. Rome was not built in a day.

Lose an hour in the morning and you'll be looking for it all day.

Wisdom

Wisdom is the comb given to a man after he has lost his hair.

Continual cheerfulness is a sign of wisdom.

Three best to have in plenty: sunshine, wisdom, and generosity.

A hint is sufficient for the wise.

You won't learn to swim on the kitchen floor.

If you give the loan of your britches, don't cut off the buttons.

The borrowed horse has hard hoofs.

Health's doctor is sleep.

Everyone lays a burden on the willing horse.

If you don't want flour on your clothes, stay out of the mill.

The man who loves danger shall perish in it.

A little fire that warms is better than a big fire that burns.

Blow not on dead embers.

The world would not make a racehorse of a donkey.

There are no unmixed blessings in life.

The little fish feed the big fish.

A bad egg, a bad bird.

A rolling stone gathers no moss.

Things aren't as they seem.

Put silk on a goat and it's still a goat.

A light heart lives long.

If it's drowning you're after, don't torment yourself with shallow water.

There is no strength without unity.

The skin of the old sheep is on the rafter no sooner than the skin of the young sheep.

Honey is sweet, but don't lick it off a briar.

Better be sparing at first than at last.

If you buy what you don't need, you might have to sell what you do.

A lock is better than suspicion.

Listen to the sound of the river and you will get a trout.

Be neither intimate nor distant with the clergy.

It is better to exist unknown to the law.

Do not take the thatch from your own roof to buy
    slates for another man's house.

A good laugh and a long sleep are the two best cures.

There is no luck except where there is discipline.

The man with the boots does not mind where he
    places his foot.

Your feet will bring you to where your heart is.

The lesson learned by a tragedy is a lesson never
    forgotten.

Long churning makes bad butter.

The wearer best knows where the shoe pinches.

Enough and no waste is as good as a feast.

There's no need to fear the wind if your haystacks
are tied down.

A good retreat is better than a bad stand.

God is good, but never dance in a small boat.

Never scald your lips with another man's porridge.

Never sell a hen on a wet day.

Keep in with the bad man for the good man won't
harm you.

Don't be breaking your shin on a stool that's not in
your way.

Wide is the door of the little cottage.

Show the fatted calf, but not the thing that fattened
him.

Don't make little of your dish for it may be an
ignorant fellow who judges it.

Words and Gossip

Where the tongue slips, it speaks the truth.

Who gossips with you will gossip of you.

A story without an author is not worth listening to.

It is not a secret if it is known by three people.

Tell it to Mary in a whisper, and Mary will tell it to
the parish.

She has a tongue that would clip a hedge. (Said of a
gossip.)

Talk by the fire is the talk of idle women.

He is scant of news that speaks ill of his mother.

Don't bless with the tip of your tongue if there's
bile at the butt.

A good word never broke a tooth.

A kind word never broke anyone's mouth. But
many times a man's mouth has broken his nose.

It is often that a person's mouth broke his nose.

Mere words do not feed the friars.

There is no tax on talk.

Work

It is a third of the work to begin.

About evening a man is known.

A trade not properly learned is an enemy.

It is a bad hen that does not scratch for itself.

Laziness is a heavy burden.

Don't let the grass grow under your feet.

If you do not sow in the spring, you will not reap in the autumn.

You'll never plough a field by turning it over in your mind.

Little as a wren needs, it must gather it.

Work without end is housewife's work.

A foot at rest means nothing.

Poverty waits at the gates of idleness.

Two thirds of the work is the semblance.

A handful of skill is better than a bagful of gold.

Do your own job and eat your own fruits.

Put it on your shoulder and say it is not a burden.

The back must slave to feed the belly.

The work praises the man.

It is the good horse that draws its own cart.

The dog that's always on the go is better than the
    one that's always curled up.

Youth

Youth does not mind where it sets its foot.

Youth likes to wander.

Praise the young and they will blossom.

You cannot put an old head on the young.

Youth cannot believe.

Youth sheds many a skin. The steed does not retain
its speed forever.

CHAPTER SIX

Poetry and Rhymes

Not only do the Irish have a way with words, but they also are quite accomplished rhymesters. They appreciate the fact that sometimes a proverb or insightful witticism sounds better in poem form or with an engaging rhyme scheme.

Me darlin' was sweet, me darlin' was chaste
Faith, an' more's the pity.
For though she was sweet an' though she was
    chaste,
She was chased all the way through the city.

—*Anonymous Irish verse, circa 1790*

Let schoolmasters puzzle their brain,
The great Gaels of Ireland
Are the men that God made mad.
For all their wars are merry,
And all their songs are sad.

—*G. K. Chesterton*

Garlic with May butter
    Cureth all disease.
    Drink of goat's white milk
        Take along with these.

—*Theodora Fitzgibbon*

With grammar, and nonsense, and learning.
Good liquor, I stoutly maintain,
Gives genius a better discerning.

—*Oliver Goldsmith*

You've heard of St. Denis of France,
He never had much for to brag on.
You've heard of St. George and his lance,
Who killed old heathenish dragon.
The Saints of the Welshmen and Scot
Are a couple of pitiful pipers,
And might just as well go to pot
When compared to the patron of vipers:
St. Patrick of Ireland, my dear.

—*William Maginn*

O long life to the man who invented potheen,
Sure the Pope ought to make him a martyr.
If myself was this moment Victoria, the Queen,
I'd drink nothing but whiskey and wather.

—*Michael Moran*

Here's to the maiden of bashful fifteen,
Here's to the widow of fifty,
Here's to the flaunting, extravagant queen,
And here's to the housewife that's thrifty!
Let the toast pass,
Drink to the lass,
I'll warrant she'll prove an excuse for the glass.

—Richard Brinsley Sheridan

There is in every cook's opinion
No savory dish without an onion.
But lest your kissing should be spoiled,
The onion must be thoroughly boiled.

—Jonathan Swift

He Wished for the Cloths of Heaven

Had I the heavens' embroidered cloths,
Enwrought with golden and silver light,
The blue and the dim and the dark cloths
Of night and light and the half-light,
I would spread the cloths under your feet.
But I, being poor, have only my dreams,
I have spread my dreams under your feet,
Tread softly because you tread on my dreams.

—William Butler Yeats

A statesman is an easy man, he tells his lies by rote.
A journalist invents his lies, and rams them down
    your throat.
So stay at home and drink your beer and let the
    neighbors vote.

—William Butler Yeats

Wine comes in at the mouth
And love comes in at the eye.
That's all that we will know for truth
Before we grow old and die.
I lift the glass to my mouth,
I look at you and I sigh.

—*William Butler Yeats*

God grant me the serenity to accept
The things I cannot change,
The strength to change the things I can,
And the wisdom to hide the bodies
Of those who pissed me off.

In all this world, why I do think
There are five reasons why we drink:
Good friends, good wine,
Lest we be dry
And any other reason why.

He's a fool who give over the liquor,
It softens the skinflint at once,
It urges the slow coach on quicker,
Gives spirit and brains to the dunce.

Drink is the curse of the land.
It makes you fight with your neighbor.
It makes you shoot at your landlord.
And it makes you miss him!

He that buys land buys many stones,
He that buys flesh buys many bones,
He that buys eggs buys many shells,
But he that buys good beer buys nothing else.

You guys came by to have some fun.
You'll come and stay all night, I fear.
But I know how to make you run.
I'll serve you all generic beer.

Champagne costs too much,
Whiskey's too rough,
Vodka puts big mouths in gear.
This little refrain
Should help to explain
Why it's better to order a beer!

When money's tight and hard to get
And your horse is also ran,
When all you have is a heap of debt
A pint of plain is your only man.

But if at church they give some ale
And a pleasant fire for our souls to regale,
We'd sing and we'd pray all the live long day
Nor ever once from the church to stray.

A limerick packs laughs anatomical
Into space that is quite economical.
But the good ones I've seen
So seldom are clean
And the clean ones so seldom are comical.

The horse and mule live thirty years
And never knows of wines and beers.
The goat and sheep at twenty die
Without a taste of scotch or rye.
The cow drinks water by the ton
And at eighteen is mostly done.
The dog at fifteen cashes in
Without the aid of rum or gin.
The modest, sober, bone-dry hen
Lays eggs for noggs and dies at ten.
But sinful, ginful, rum-soaked men
Survive three-score years and ten.
And some of us . . . though mighty few
Stay pickled 'til we're ninety-two.

The man who is dumb as a rule
Discovers a great deal to say,
While he who is bashful since Yule
Will talk in an amorous way.

It's drink that uplifts the poltroon
To give battle in France and in Spain,
Now here is an end of my turn
And fill me that bumper again!

Irish Curses, Blessings, and Toasts

Nary a day goes by that I miss to wonder why
The moon shows his face as the day draws nigh.
In the firelight I ponder my canine's thought
As he gazes upon me from his hand-me-down cot.
I think of God and all his creations,
One being the woman with her unbridled tempta-
    tions.
I have searched for love with no direction,
skeletons in the closet . . . a fine collection.
These quandaries of mine, I'm sure to figure out.
For I know the answer lies at the bottom of this
    stout.

Of all my favorite things to do,
The utmost is to have a brew.
My love grows for my foamy friend,
With each thirst-quenching elbow bend.
Beer's so frothy, smooth, and cold–
It's paradise–pure liquid gold.
Yes, beer means many things to me . . .
That's all for now, I gotta pee!

Tax his tractor, tax his mule, tell him, taxing is the
   rule.
Tax his oil, tax his gas, tax his
   notes, tax his cash.
Tax him good and let him
   know, that after taxes,
   he has no dough.
If he hollers, tax him more, tax him
   till he's good and sore.
Tax his coffin, tax his grave, tax his sod in which
   he's laid.
Put these words upon his tomb, "Taxes drove him
   to his doom."
Once he's gone, we won't relax. We'll still collect
   inheritance tax.

Practice makes perfect,
There's many do think,
But a man's not too perfect
When he's practiced at drink.

CHAPTER SEVEN

He Said, She Said

The original authors of so many of the Irish proverbs, assorted sayings, and witticisms are unknown. But there are many men and women of Irish descent from the past and present—writers, actors, comedians, politicians, et al.—who are both renowned and quotable. This eclectic roster of personages is regularly quoted at parties, in pubs, and on all kinds of occasions.

Dave Barry, author and humorist,
1947-

Without question, the greatest invention in the history of mankind is beer. Oh, I grant you that the wheel was also a fine invention, but the wheel does not go nearly as well with pizza.

I like beer. On occasion, I will even drink beer to celebrate a major event such as the fall of communism or the fact that the refrigerator is still working.

Irish Curses, Blessings, and Toasts

Samuel Beckett, novelist and playwright, 1906–1989

Ever tried. Ever failed. No matter. Try again. Fail again. Fail better.

I have my faults, but changing my tune is not one of them.

Personally, I have no bone to pick with graveyards.

Birth was the death of him.

What do I know of man's destiny? I could tell you more about radishes.

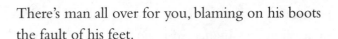

There's man all over for you, blaming on his boots the fault of his feet.

We are all born mad. Some remain so.

Brendan Behan, novelist and playwright, 1923-1964

There is no such thing as bad publicity except your own obituary.

A man is already halfway in love with anybody who listens to him.

If it was raining soup, the Irish would go out with forks.

No yesterdays are ever wasted for those that give themselves to today.

No man can discover his own talents.

I was court-martialed in my absence and sentenced to death in my absence, so I said they could shoot me in my absence.

Every man, through fear, mugs his aspirations a dozen times a day.

I saw a notice that said "Drink Canada Dry" and I've just started.

It's a good deed to forget a poor joke.

One drink is too many for me and a thousand not enough.

It's not that the Irish are cynical. It's rather that they have a wonderful lack of respect for everything and everybody.

Shakespeare said pretty well everything and what he left out, James Joyce, with a judge from meself, put in.

Kenneth Branagh, actor and director, 1960–

Lighten up, just enjoy life, smile more, laugh more, and don't get so worked up about things.

If it's good art, it's good.

It's quite hard for people to just accept that they're very contradictory.

A brother who is unhappy is a dangerous relative to have.

Life is surreal and beautiful.

You can't live in nostalgia-land.

 Life is about making plans from which you deviate, almost always. If you are lucky, you do come up with a plan.

One of the problems with Shakespeare is that you can never give him a ring.

Gabriel Byrne, actor and director, 1950–

I think there's a bit of the devil in everybody. There's a bit of a priest in everybody, too, but I enjoyed playing the devil more. He was more fun.

Richard J. Daley, Irish-American politician, 1902-1976

No man is an Ireland.

Power is dangerous unless you have humility.

The police are not here to create disorder. They're here to preserve disorder.

J. P. Donleavy, novelist and playwright, 1926-

When I die, I want to decompose in a barrel of porter and have it served in all the pubs in Dublin. I wonder would they know it was me?

To marry the Irish is to look for poverty.

Writing is turning one's worst moments into money.

F. Scott Fitzgerald, novelist,
1896–1940

There are only the pursued, the pursuing, the busy and the tired.

Everybody's youth is a dream, a form of chemical madness.

First you take a drink, then the drink takes a drink, then the drink takes you.

Personality is an unbroken series of successful gestures.

Nothing is as obnoxious as other people's luck.

Show me a hero and I'll write you a tragedy.

The victor belongs to the spoils.

To a profound pessimist about life, being in danger is not depressing.

Never confuse a single defeat with a final defeat.

Action is character.

No such thing as a man willing to be honest—that would be like a blind man willing to see.

It's not a slam at you when people are rude, it's a slam at the people they've met before.

John Fletcher, playwright, 1579–1625

Best while you have it use your breath, there is no drinking after death.

He is never alone that is accompanied with noble thoughts.

Love's tongue is in the eyes.

Drink today and drown all sorrow, you shall perhaps not do tomorrow.

Deeds, not words, shall speak me.

Oliver Goldsmith, novelist and playwright, 1728-1774

When any one of our relations was found to be a person of a very bad character, a troublesome guest, or one we desired to get rid of, upon his leaving my house I ever took care to lend him a riding-coat, or a pair of boots, or sometimes a horse of small value, and I always had the satisfaction of finding he never came back to return them.

I chose my wife as she did her wedding gown. For qualities that would wear well.

The company of fools may first make us smile, but in the end we all feel melancholy.

Hope is such a bait. It covers any hook.

Tenderness is a virtue.

Every absurdity has a champion to defend it.

A great source of calamity lies in regret and anticipation; therefore a person is wise who thinks of the
present alone, regardless of the past or future.

Pity and friendship are two passions incompatible
with each other.

Surely the best way to meet the enemy is head on
in the field and not wait till they plunder our very
homes.

They say women and music should never be dated.

Law grinds the poor and rich men
rule the law.

You can breach a better
sermon with your life than
with your lips.

Richard Harris, actor and singer, 1930-2002

I formed a new group called Alcoholics Unanimous. If you don't feel like a drink, you ring another member and he comes over to persuade you.

They'd go to the opening of an envelope. Any big occasion, they're always there. Anything for exposure. We can do without them. Actors are unimportant.

There's more fiction in my life than in books, so I don't bother with them.

I often sit back and think, I wish I'd done that, and find out later that I already have.

James Joyce, novelist, 1882–1941

Christopher Columbus, as everyone knows, is honored by posterity because he was the last to discover America.

A man of genius makes no mistakes; his errors are volitional and are the portals of discovery.

The actions of men are the best interpreters of their thoughts.

Ireland sober is Ireland stiff.

Ireland is the old sow that eats her farrow.

Better pass boldly into that other world, in the full glory of some passion, than fade and wither dismally with age.

Irresponsibility is part of the pleasure of all art. It is the part the schools cannot recognize.

Whatever else is unsure in this stinking dunghill of a world, a mother's love is not.

Shakespeare is the happy hunting ground of all minds that have lost their balance.

God spoke to you by so many voices but you would not hear.

John F. Kennedy, Irish-American politician, 1917-1963

History is a relentless master. It has no present, only the past rushing into the future. To try to hold fast is to be swept aside.

We don't want to be like the leader in the French Revolution who said: "There go my people. I must find out where they are going so I can lead them."

Change is the law of life. And those who look only to the past or present are certain to miss the future.

Leadership and learning are indispensable to each other.

Those who make peaceful revolution impossible will make violent revolution inevitable.

Efforts and courage are not enough without purpose and direction.

We must use time as a tool, not as a couch.

When power leads man toward arrogance, poetry reminds him of his limitations. When power narrows the area of man's concern, poetry reminds him of the richness and diversity of existence. When power corrupts, poetry cleanses.

The greater our knowledge increases, the more our ignorance unfolds.

A man may die, nations may rise and fall, but an idea lives on.

Forgive your enemies, but never forget their names.

Things do not happen. Things are made to happen.

The time to repair the roof is when the sun is shining.

Once you say you're going to settle for second, that's what happens to you in life.

The courage of life is often a less dramatic spectacle than the courage of a final moment, but it is no less a magnificent mixture of triumph and tragedy.

Hugh Kenner, literary critic, 1923–2003

Definition of an "Irish fact": That which tells you not what is the case but what you want to hear.

Irish Curses, Blessings, and Toasts

Hugh Leonard, writer and essayist, 1926-2009

My grandmother made dying her life's work.

We are all the foolishness and all crimes that we did. We're also all the kindnesses we did. I hate to think of life as if we understood time. We don't understand time.

The problem with Ireland is that it's a country full of genius, but with absolutely no talent.

I've always enjoyed a woman's company more than men's. They're usually better looking.

All I ever seemed to get was the kind of girl who had a special dispensation from Rome to wear the thickest part of her legs below the knee.

An Irishman will always soften bad news, so that a major coronary is no more than "a bad turn" and a near hurricane that leaves thousands homeless is "good drying weather."

A thing well done is worth doing.

Gossip is more popular than literature.

My life is every moment of my life. It is not a culmination of the past.

Shane Leslie, writer and diplomat, 1885-1971

Every St. Patrick's Day every Irishman goes out to find another Irishman to make a speech to.

It is a pledge that senility has not the last say in everything.

C.S. Lewis, novelist, 1898-1963

Courage is not simply one of the virtues, but the form of every virtue at the testing point.

Education without values, as useful as it is, seems rather to make man a more clever devil.

Failures, repeated failures, are finger posts on the road to achievement. One fails forward toward success.

If the whole universe has no meaning, we should never have found out that it has no meaning. Just as, if there were no light in the universe, and therefore no creatures with eyes, we should never know it was dark. Dark would be without meaning.

It may be hard for an egg to turn into a bird. It would be a jolly sight harder for it to learn to fly while remaining an egg. We are like eggs at present. And you cannot go on indefinitely being just an ordinary, decent egg. We must be hatched or go bad.

Nothing that you have not given away will ever be really yours.

Don't use words too big for the subject. Don't say 'infinitely' when you mean 'very,' otherwise you'll have no word left when you want to talk about something really infinite.

Let's pray that the human race never escapes from Earth to spread its iniquity elsewhere.

With the possible exception of the equator, everything begins somewhere.

The future is something which everyone reaches at the rate of sixty minutes an hour, whatever he does, whoever he is.

Friendship is unnecessary, like philosophy, like art. It has no survival value. Rather, it is one of those things that give value to survival.

Robert Wilson Lynd, writer and essayist, 1879-1949

I am a confirmed believer in blessings in disguise. I prefer them undisguised when I myself happen to be the person blessed; in fact, I can scarcely recognize a blessing in disguise except when it is bestowed upon someone else.

There is nothing in which the birds differ more from man than the way in which they can build and yet leave a landscape as it was before.

It is almost impossible to remember how tragic a place the world is when one is playing golf.

No human being believes that any other human being has a right to be in bed when he himself is up.

Every man of genius is considerably helped by being dead.

Most human beings are quite likeable if you do not see too much of them.

John Pentland Mahaffy, writer and scholar, 1839–1919

In Ireland the inevitable never happens and the unexpected constantly occurs.

Never tell a story because it is true. Tell it because it is a good story.

Colum McCann, novelist,
1965-

The thing about love is that we come alive in bodies not our own.

Irish Curses, Blessings, and Toasts

Danny McGoorty, pool hustler
and billiards champion,
?–1970

One of the worst things that can happen in life is to win a bet on a horse at an early age.

I have never liked working. To me a job is an invasion of privacy.

Mignon McLaughlin, journalist and author, 1913–1983

A successful marriage requires falling in love many times, always with the same person.

Hope is the feeling we have that the feeling we have is not permanent.

Love unlocks doors and opens windows that weren't even there before.

It's the most unhappy people who most fear change.

No one really listens to anyone else, and if you try it for a while you'll see why.

Even cowards can endure hardship; only the brave can endure suspense.

A sense of humor is a major defense against minor troubles.

For the happiest life, days should be rigorously planned, nights left open to chance.

It's innocence when it charms us, ignorance when it doesn't.

Our strength is often composed of the weakness that we're damned if we're going to show.

The young are generally full of revolt, and are often pretty revolting about it.

There are so many things that we wish we had done yesterday, so few that we feel like doing today.

Courage can't see around corners but goes around them anyway.

Youth is not enough. And love is not enough. And success is not enough. And, if we could achieve it, enough would not be enough.

Every society honors its live conformists and its dead troublemakers.

The only mothers it is safe to forget on Mother's Day are the good ones.

The proud man can learn humility, but he will be proud of it.

Irish Curses, Blessings, and Toasts

Christopher Meloni, actor, 1961-

My first thought when I came [to Ireland] was that I understood why there are so many great Irish writers—because there is something mystical in the air. There's always this cloudy, moody sky and it's challenging.

Spike Milligan, actor, writer, playwright, comedian, 1918-2002

My father had a profound influence on me; he was a lunatic.

Are you going to come quietly, or do I have to use earplugs?

All I ask is the chance to prove that money can't make me happy.

A sure cure for seasickness is to sit under a tree.

Money can't buy you happiness, but it does bring you a more pleasant form of misery.

Money couldn't buy friends, but you got a better class of enemy.

And God said, "Let there be light" and there was light, but the Electricity Board said He would have to wait until Thursday to be connected.

Marianne Moore, poet,
1887–1972

I'm troubled. I'm dissatisfied. I'm Irish.

Daniel Patrick Moynihan, Irish–American politician, 1927-2003

Everyone is entitled to his own opinion, but not his own facts.

The single most exciting thing you encounter in government is competence, because it's so rare.

To be Irish is to know that in the end the world will break your heart.

Iris Murdoch, novelist and philosopher, 1919–1999

I think being a woman is like being Irish. Everyone says you're important and nice, but you take second place all the same.

Love is the difficult realization that something other than oneself is real.

Falling out of love is chiefly a matter of forgetting how charming someone is.

Between saying and doing, many a pair of shoes is worn out.

People from a planet without flowers would think we must be mad with joy the whole time to have such things about us.

We live in a fantasy world, a world of illusion. The great task in life is to find reality.

Every man needs two women: a quiet homemaker and a thrilling nymph.

One doesn't have to get anywhere in a marriage. It's not a public conveyance.

Edna O'Brien, novelist and playwright, 1930-

The vote means nothing to women. We should be armed.

In our deepest moments, we say the most inadequate things.

Darkness is drawn to light, but light does not know it; light must absorb the darkness and therefore meet its own extinguishment.

We all leave one another. We die, we change—it's mostly change—we outgrow our best friends; but even if I do leave you, I will have passed on to you something of myself; you will be a different person because of knowing me; it's inescapable.

Sean O'Casey, playwright, 1880-1964

The hallway of every man's life is paced with pictures; pictures gay and pictures gloomy, all useful, for if we be wise, we can learn from them a richer and braver way to live.

Money does not make you happy but it quiets the nerves.

It's my rule never to lose me temper till it would be detrimental to keep it.

All the world's a stage and most of us are desperately unrehearsed.

That's the Irish people all over. They treat a joke as a serious thing and a serious thing as a joke.

No man is so old to believe he cannot live one more year.

Austin O'Malley, professor of English literature, 1858–1932

An Irishman can be worried by the consciousness that there is nothing to worry about.

Revenge is often like biting a dog because the dog bit you.

Happiness is the harvest of a quiet eye.

A pint of sweat will save a gallon of blood.

If you keep your mouth shut, you will never put your foot in it.

Eugene O'Neill, playwright,
1888–1953

There is no present or future—only
the past, happening over and over
again now.

Life is for each man a solitary
cell whose walls are mirrors.

When men make gods, there is
no God!

When you're fifty you start thinking about things
you haven't thought about before. I used to think
getting old was about vanity—but actually it's about
losing people you love. Getting wrinkles is trivial.

Man's loneliness is but his fear of life.

Brian O'Nolan (Flann O'Brien), novelist and playwright, 1911–1966

The majority of the members of the Irish parliament are professional politicians, in the sense that otherwise they would not be given jobs minding mice at crossroads.

Rome wasn't built in A.D.

Remember that I too was Irish. Today I am cured. I am no longer Irish. I am merely a person. I cured myself after many years of suffering.

John Boyle O'Reilly, journalist and poet, 1844–1890

Ireland is a fruitful mother of genius, but a barren nurse.

The right word fitly spoken is a precious rarity.

Irish Curses, Blessings, and Toasts

P. J. O'Rourke, journalist and political satirist, 1947–

You know your children are growing up when they stop asking you where they came from and refuse to tell you where they're going.

Not much was really invented during the Renaissance, if you don't count modern civilization.

Never wear anything that panics the cat.

Never serve oysters in a month that has no paycheck in it.

There is a remarkable breakdown of taste and intelligence at Christmastime. Mature, responsible grown men wear neckties made of holly leaves and drink alcoholic beverages with raw egg yolks in them.

Humans are the only animals that have children on purpose with the exception of guppies, who like to eat theirs.

Family love is messy, clinging, and of an annoying and repetitive pattern, like bad wallpaper.

Each child is biologically required to have a mother. Fatherhood is a well-regarded theory, but motherhood is a fact.

Ending wars is very simple if you surrender.

Earnestness is stupidity sent to college.

Seriousness is stupidity sent to college.

Always read something that will make you look good if you die in the middle of it.

A fruit is a vegetable with looks and money. Plus, if you let fruit rot, it turns into wine, something Brussels sprouts never do.

Peter O'Toole, actor, 1932–2013

My favorite food from my homeland is Guinness. My second choice is Guinness. My third choice would have to be Guinness.

When I work with young people, I grab energy from them by the handful.

The only exercise I take is walking behind the coffins of friends who took exercise.

Irish women are always carrying water on their heads, and always carrying their husbands home from pubs. Such things are the greatest posture-builders in the world.

The common denominator of all my friends is that they're dead.

If you can't do something willingly and joyfully, then don't do it.

If I'd known I was going to live this long, I would have taken better care of myself.

Hal Roach, comedian, 1927–2012

You know it's summer in Ireland when the rain gets warmer.

Boyle Roche, Irish politician, 1736-1807

The cup of Ireland's misery has been overflowing for centuries and is not yet half full.

All along the untrodden paths of the future, I can see the footprints of an unseen hand.

Why should we do anything for posterity? What has posterity done for us?

The best way to avoid danger is to meet it plump.

The only thing to prevent what's past is to put a stop to it before it happens.

Every pint bottle should contain a quart.

George Bernard Shaw, playwright,
1856–1950

I often quote myself. It adds spice to my conversation.

Life is no brief candle to me. It is a sort of splendid torch, which I have got a hold of for the moment, and I want to make it burn as brightly as possible before handing it on to future generations.

You use a glass mirror to see your face. You use works of art to see your soul.

Newspapers are unable, seemingly, to discriminate between a bicycle accident and the collapse of civilization.

The only man I know who behaves sensibly is my tailor. He takes my measurements anew each time he sees me. The rest go on with their old measurements and expect me to fit them.

Except during the nine months before he draws his first breath, no man manages his affairs as well as a tree does.

A life making mistakes is not only more honorable, but more useful than a life spent doing nothing at all.

First love is only a little foolishness and a lot of curiosity.

Man can climb the highest summits, but he cannot dwell there long.

The reasonable man adapts himself to the world; the unreasonable one persists in trying to adapt the world to himself.

Put an Irishman on the spit and you can always get another Irishman to turn him.

Do not do unto others as you would that they should do unto you; their tastes may not be the same.

Nothing is ever done in this world until men are prepared to kill one another if it is not done.

If you cannot get rid of the family skeleton, you may as well make it dance.

The government which robs Peter to pay Paul can always depend on the support of Paul.

The fickleness of the women I love is only equaled by the infernal constancy of the women who love me.

The trouble with her is that she lacks the power of conversation but not the power of speech.

My way of joking is to tell the truth. It's the funniest joke in the world.

To be clever enough to get a great deal of money, one must be stupid enough to want it.

Nothing soothes me more after a long and maddening course of pianoforte recitals than to sit and have my teeth drilled.

Few people think more than two or three times a year. I have made an international reputation for myself by thinking once or twice a week.

He knows nothing and and he thinks he knows everything. That points clearly to a political career.

If all economists were laid end to end, they would not reach a conclusion.

Patriotism is your conviction that this country is superior to all other countries because you were born in it.

I'm only a beer teetotaler, not a champagne teetotaler.

Richard Brinsley Sheridan, playwright and satirist, 1751–1816

Be just before you are generous.

The surest way to fail is not to determine to succeed.

I mean, the question actors most often get asked is how they can bear saying the same things over and over again, night after night. But God knows the answer to that is: Don't we all anyway—might as well get paid for it.

There is not a passion so strongly rooted in the human heart than envy.

A bumper of good liquor will end a contest quicker than a justice, judge, or vicar.

Those that vow the most are the least sincere.

There is no possibility of being witty without a little ill-nature.

Jonathan Swift, satirist and essayist, 1667–1745

Every dog must have his day.

The proper words in the proper places are the true definition of style.

It was a bold man who first swallowed an oyster.

A tavern is a place where madness is sold by the bottle.

Vision is the art of seeing what is invisible to others.

There is nothing constant in this world but inconsistency.

Blessed is he who expects nothing, for he shall never be disappointed.

No wise man ever wished to be younger.

One enemy can do more hurt than ten friends can do good.

Don't set your wit against a child.

Nothing is so hard for those who abound in riches as to conceive how others can be in want.

Every man desires to live long, but no man wishes to be old.

John Millington Synge, playwright, 1871–1909

There is no language like the Irish for soothing and quieting.

A man who is not afraid of the sea will soon be drowned.

Katharine Tynan, novelist and poet, 1861–1931

There is an Irish way of paying compliments
as though they were irresistible truths, which
makes what would otherwise be an impertinence
delightful.

The way with Ireland is that no sooner do you get
away from her than the golden mists begin to close
about her, and she lies, an Island of the Blest, something enchanted in our dreams. When you come
back you may think you are disillusioned, but you
know well that the fairy mists will begin to gather
about her once more.

The life in which nothing happens goes the fastest, because it has no landmarks.

Hope is at the bottom of the Pandora's box of Irish troubles.

Irish people have a trick of over-statement, at which one ceases to wince as one grows older.

I have often heard it said that the Irish are too ready to forgive. It is a noble failing.

The Irish always jest even though they jest with tears.

Oscar Wilde, novelist and playwright, 1854–1900

Yes, I am a dreamer. For a dreamer is one who can only find his way by moonlight, and his punishment is that he sees the dawn before the rest of the world.

A little sincerity is a dangerous thing, and a great deal of it is absolutely fatal.

I can resist everything except temptation.

The only way to get rid of a temptation is to yield to it.

To love oneself is the beginning of a lifelong romance.

After a good dinner, one can forgive anybody, even one's own relations.

Always forgive your enemies; nothing annoys them so much.

I choose my friends for their good looks, my acquaintances for their good characters, and my enemies for their good intellects. A man cannot be too careful in the choice of his enemies.

It is absurd to divide people into good and bad. People are either charming or tedious.

True friends stab you in the front.

What is a cynic? A man who knows the price of everything and the value of nothing.

Democracy means simply the bludgeoning of the people, by the people, for the people.

The difference between literature and journalism is that journalism is unreadable and literature is unread.

The truth is rarely pure and never simple.

Work is the curse of the drinking classes.

Experience is the name everyone gives to their mistakes.

My own business always bores me to death; I prefer other people's.

Life is far too important a thing ever to talk seriously about.

Death must be so beautiful. To lie in the soft brown earth, with the grasses waving above one's head, and listen to silence. To have no yesterday, and no tomorrow. To forget time, to forgive life, to be at peace.

When the gods wish to punish us, they answer our prayers.

I think that God in creating Man somewhat overestimated his ability.

The only thing worse than being talked about is not being talked about.

Whenever people agree with me I always feel I must be wrong.

If you want to tell people the truth, make them laugh, otherwise they'll kill you.

Some cause happiness wherever they go; others whenever they go.

It is always a silly thing to give advice, but to give good advice is fatal.

One should always play fairly when one has the winning cards.

Patriotism is the virtue of the vicious.

The only thing to do with good advice is pass it on. It is never any use to oneself.

The only thing that can console one for being poor is extravagance.

A man's face is his autobiography. A woman's face is her work of fiction.

Biography lends to death a new terror.

A sentimentalist is simply one who desires to have the luxury of an emotion without paying for it.

To make a good salad is to be a brilliant diplomatist—the problem is entirely the same in both cases: To know exactly how much oil one must put with one's vinegar.

I dislike arguments of any kind. They are always vulgar, and often convincing.

A man who moralizes is usually a hypocrite, and a woman who moralizes is usually plain.

Fashion is a form of ugliness so intolerable that we have to alter it every six months.

I am not young enough to know everything.

I often take exercise. Only yesterday I had breakfast in bed.

Anyone who lives within their means suffers from a lack of imagination.

Moderation is a fatal thing. Nothing succeeds like excess.

America had often been discovered before Columbus, but it had always been hushed up.

We are all of us in the gutter. But some of us are looking at the stars.

Anybody can make history.
Only a great man can write it.

I must decline your invitation owing to a subsequent engagement.

She who hesitates is won.

No woman should ever be quite accurate about her age. It looks so calculating.

I never put off till tomorrow what I can do the day after.

Children begin by loving their parents. After a time they judge them. Rarely, if ever, do they forgive them.

All women become like their mothers. That is their tragedy. No man does. That's his.

I should imagine that most mothers don't quite understand their sons.

Bigamy is having one wife too many. Marriage is the same.

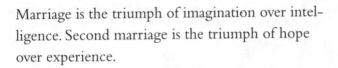

The proper basis for marriage is mutual misunderstanding.

Marriage is the triumph of imagination over intelligence. Second marriage is the triumph of hope over experience.

I like men who have a future and women who have a past.

As long as war is regarded as wicked, it will always have its fascination. When it is looked upon as vulgar, it will cease to be popular.

William Butler Yeats, poet, 1865–1939

The problem with some people is that when they aren't drunk, they're sober.

Life seems to me a preparation for something that never happens.

Being Irish, I have an abiding sense of tragedy, which sustains me through temporary periods of joy.

Do not wait to strike till the iron is hot, but make it hot by striking.

Chapter Eight

Ballads and Folk Songs

The Irish are renowned for their ballads and folk songs, which, in many instances, have been passed down through generations. Typically, they impart a pithy story with an accompanying melody appropriate for the subject matter. Many ballads and folk songs are historical and chronicle the likes of war, revolution, and soldiers on the frontlines. Some are poignant and recount tales of love, romance, and parting. Of course, there are also drinking ballads and folk songs, quite moving in some cases and hysterically funny in others.

The Parting Glass
(favorite parting song)

Of all the money that e'er I spent,
I've spent it in good company.
And all the harm that ever I did,
Alas it was to none but me.
And all I've done for want of wit
To memory now I can't recall.
So fill to me the parting glass,
Good night and joy be with you all.

If I had money enough to spend
And leisure to sit awhile,
There is a fair maid in the town
That sorely has my heart beguiled.
Her rosy cheeks and ruby lips
I own she has my heart enthralled.
So fill to me the parting glass,
Good night and joy be with you all.

Oh, all the comrades that e'er I had,
They're sorry for my going away.
And all the sweethearts that e'er I had,
They'd wish me one more day to stay.
But since it falls unto my lot
That I should rise and you should not,
I'll gently rise and softly call,
Good night and joy be with you all.

She Moved Through the Fair
(traditional Irish folk song)

My young love said to me, my mother won't mind,
And my father won't slight you for your lack of
    kine (cows).
And she stepped away from me and this she did say,
It will not be long love 'til our wedding day.

She stepped away from me and she moved through
   the fair,
And fondly I watched her move here and move
    there.
Then she went her way homeward with one star
    awake,
As the swan in the evening moves over the lake.

The people were saying no two were e'er wed,
But one has a sorrow that never was said.
And I smiled as she passed with her goods and her
    gear,
And that was the last that I saw of my dear.

I dreamt it last night that my young love came in,
So softly she entered her feet made no din.
She came close beside me and this she did say,
It will not be long love 'til our wedding day.

The Wild Rover

I've been a wild rover for many a year
And I spent all my money on whiskey and beer.
And now I'm returning with gold in great store
And I never will play the wild rover no more.

And it's no, nay, never,
No, nay, never, no more,
Will I play the wild rover,
No, never, no more.

I went to an alehouse I used to frequent
And I told the landlady my money was spent.
I asked her for credit, she answered me "Nay,
Such a custom as yours I could have any day."

And it's no, nay, never,
No, nay, never, no more,
Will I play the wild rover,
No, never, no more.

I took from my pocket ten sovereigns bright
And the landlady's eyes opened wide with delight.
She said, "I have whiskey and wines of the best
And the words that I spoke sure were only in jest."

And it's no, nay, never,
No, nay, never, no more,
Will I play the wild rover,
No, never, no more.

I'll go home to my parents, confess what I've done
And I'll ask them to pardon their prodigal son.
And if they caress me as oft times before
Sure I never will play the wild rover no more.

And it's no, nay, never,
No, nay, never, no more,
Will I play the wild rover,
No, never, no more.

Molly Malone (unofficial anthem of Dublin)

In Dublin's fair city,
Where girls are so pretty,
I first set my eyes on sweet Molly Malone,
As she pushed her wheelbarrow
Through streets broad and narrow,
Crying, "Cockles and mussels, alive, alive oh!"

Alive, alive oh! alive, alive oh!
Crying, "Cockles and mussels, alive, alive oh!"

Now she was a fishmonger,
And sure 'twas no wonder,
For so were her mother and father before,
And they each wheeled their barrow,
Through streets broad and narrow,
Crying, "Cockles and mussels, alive, alive oh!"

Alive, alive oh! alive, alive oh!
Crying, "Cockles and mussels, alive, alive oh!"

She died of a fever,
And no one could save her,
And that was the end of sweet Molly Malone.
Now her ghost wheels her barrow,
Through streets broad and narrow,
Crying, "Cockles and mussels, alive, alive oh!"

Alive, alive oh! alive, alive oh!
Crying, "Cockles and mussels, alive, alive oh!"

A Little Bit of Heaven

Sure a little bit of Heaven fell from out the sky one
    day
And it nestled in the ocean in a place so far away.
And when the angels found it sure it looked so
    sweet and fair.
They said suppose we leave it for it looks so peace-
    ful there.

So they sprinkled it with stardust just to make the
    shamrocks grow.
It's the only place you'll find them no matter where
    you go.
Then they darted it with silver just to make
    the lakes look grand
And when they had it finished sure
    they called it Ireland.

Finnegan's Wake

Tim Finnegan lived in Walkin Street, a gentle Irishman mighty odd.
He had a brogue both rich and sweet, an' to rise in
  the world he carried a hod.
You see he'd a sort of a tippler's way, but the love
  for the liquor poor Tim was born.
To help him on his way each day, he'd a drop of the
  craythur every morn.

Whack fol the dah, now dance to yer partner
  around the flure yer trotters shake.
Wasn't it the truth I told you? Lots of fun at Finnegan's Wake.

One morning Tim got rather full, his head felt
  heavy which made him shake.
Fell from a ladder and he broke his skull, and they
  carried him home his corpse to wake.
Rolled him up in a nice clean sheet, and laid him
  out upon the bed,
A bottle of whiskey at his feet and a barrel of porter
  at his head.

Whack fol the dah, now dance to yer partner
   around the flure yer trotters shake.
Wasn't it the truth I told you? Lots of fun at Finnegan's Wake.

His friends assembled at the wake, and
   Mrs. Finnegan called for lunch.
First she brought in tay and cake, then pipes,
   tobacco, and whiskey punch.
Biddy O'Brien began to cry, "Such a nice clean
   corpse, did you ever see,
Tim mavourneen, why did you die?" "Will ye
   hould your gob?" said Paddy McGee.

Whack fol the dah, now dance to yer partner
  around the flure yer trotters shake.
Wasn't it the truth I told you? Lots of fun at Finnegan's Wake.

Then Maggie O'Connor took up the job, "Biddy"
  says she "you're wrong, I'm sure."
Biddy gave her a belt in the gob and left her
  sprawling on the floor.
Then the war did soon engage, t'was woman to
  woman and man to man.
Shilellagh law was all the rage and a row and a ruction soon began.

Whack fol the dah, now dance to yer partner
  around the flure yer trotters shake.
Wasn't it the truth I told you? Lots of fun at Finnegan's Wake.

Mickey Maloney ducked his head when a bucket of
  whiskey flew at him.
It missed, and falling on the bed, the liquor scat-
  tered over Tim.

Bedad he revives, see how he rises, Timothy rising
    from the bed,
Saying, "Whittle your whiskey around like blazes,
    t'underin' Jaysus, do ye think I'm dead?"

Whack fol the dah, now dance to yer partner
    around the flure yer trotters shake.
Wasn't it the truth I told you? Lots of fun at Fin-
    negan's Wake.

Whack fol the dah, now dance to yer partner
    around the flure yer trotters shake.
Wasn't it the truth I told you? Lots of fun at Fin-
    negan's Wake.

Terms:

Hod: builder's tool for carrying bricks and assorted building materials.

Tippler: drunkard.

Craythur: whiskey.

Whack fol the dah: phrase intended to sound like an instrument.

Trotters: feet.

Full: drunk.

Mavourneen: my darling.

Hould your gob: keep your mouth closed.

Belt in the gob: a punch in the mouth.

Shilellagh law: rules for combat.

Ruction: quarrel.

Bedad: expression of surprise.

God Save Ireland
(Irish rebel song)

High upon the gallows tree swung the noble-
hearted three.
By the vengeful tyrant stricken in their bloom,
But they met him face to face, with the courage of
their race,
And they went with souls undaunted to their
doom.

"God save Ireland!" said the heroes.
"God save Ireland" said they all.
Whether on the scaffold high
Or the battlefield we die,
Oh, what matter when for Erin dear we fall!

Girt around with cruel foes, still their courage
    proudly rose,
For they thought of hearts that loved them far and
    near,
Of the millions true and brave o'er the ocean's
    swelling wave,
And the friends in holy Ireland ever dear.

"God save Ireland!" said the heroes.
"God save Ireland" said they all.
Whether on the scaffold high
Or the battlefield we die,
Oh, what matter when for Erin dear we fall!

Climbed they up the rugged stair, rang their voices
    out in prayer,
Then with England's fatal cord around them cast,

Close beside the gallows tree kissed like brothers
   lovingly,
True to home and faith and freedom to the last.

"God save Ireland!" said the heroes.
"God save Ireland" said they all.
Whether on the scaffold high
Or the battlefield we die,
Oh, what matter when for Erin dear we fall!

Never till the latest day shall the memory pass away,
Of the gallant lives thus given for our land,
But on the cause must go, amidst joy and weal
   and woe,
Till we make our Isle a nation free and grand.

Irish Curses, Blessings, and Toasts